POCKET GUIDE TO
THE
CHAKRAS

BY JOY GARDNER-GORDON

THE CROSSING PRESS
FREEDOM, CALIFORNIA

Special thanks to:

My publisher and editor, Elaine Gill, for conceptualizing the book.

My husband, Raphael Gardner-Gordon, for being my fearless editor.

My daughter-in-law, Petra Prensky, for critiquing the manuscript.

My friend, Angela Rosa, for research assistance on the aromatic oils.

My masseuse, Karen Withrow, for alleviating my aches and pains.

Copyright © 1998 by Vibrational Healing Enterprises
Interior illustration by Peggy McCarty
Printed in the U.S.A.
2nd Printing 1999

For information on bulk purchases or group discounts for this and other Crossing Press titles, please contact our Special Sales Manager at 800/777-1048.

www.crossingpress.com

Library of Congress Cataloging-in-Publication Data

Gardner-Gordon, Joy.
    Pocket guide to the chakras / Joy Gardner-Gordon.
        p. cm. -- (The Crossing Press pocket series)
    ISBN 0-89594-949-0 (pbk.)
    1. Chakras--Miscellanea. I. Title. II. Series.
    BF1442.C53G37 1998
    131--dc21   98-24642
                                                        CIP

Contents

Overview

A person with the gift of clairvoyance can see all your seven energy vortexes radiating like multi-colored suns along the axis of your spine. These whorls of spinning energy are known as *chakras*, the Sanskrit word for wheel. Until recently, in the Western world, this term was confined to esoteric groups of people, outside of which a person who claimed to see or feel the energy of the chakras might be kindly tolerated at best.

Today this ancient awareness is becoming recognized as a legitimate model for health and illness, providing us with a rich, complex method for organizing the holistic gestalt of the human body/emotions/mind/spirit.

This book is an introduction to the chakras. It is a valuable tool for the holistic practitioner and for the person who seeks a deeper level of self-knowledge. The reader will find answers to these questions:

- What are the chakras?
- Where are they?
- How do they function?
- What causes them to open or close?
- How can you change their energy?

This "Overview" includes a brief history of the chakras, where they are and what they do. It shows how the chakra system enables you to analyze the health of your body/emotions/mind/spirit and how this system can enhance your understanding of human relationships.

The section on "Development of the Chakras" explains how events influence the opening and closing of the chakras. The chapters on each of the chakras describe the use of colors, tones, crystals, and aromas that correspond to each of these seven energy centers.

"Evaluation and Treatment" describes the seven levels of openness that can occur at any given chakra, and the healing methods that make use of this system.

HISTORY OF THE CHAKRAS

Knowledge of the chakras has survived far longer than recorded history and can be found in texts and artwork throughout India, Egypt, China, Tibet, Hawaii, in various parts of Europe and Africa, and among American Indian tribes. We find the chakras described in the Vedas and the Upanishads, the ancient teachings of Hinduism. It was practiced in the ancient Greek mystery schools of Eleusis and Delphi, and by early Christian mystics and Hermetics.

In *The Aquarian Gospel of Jesus The Christ*, Levi gives a convincing argument for the education of Jesus in India, Tibet, and other parts of the Far East. In the *New Testament*, Luke 11:34, Jesus says, "The light of the body is the eye: therefore when thine eye is single, thy whole body also is full of light; but when thine eye is evil, thy body also is full of darkness." Surely he was speaking about the third eye, which is the sixth chakra, also known as the Christ Consciousness center.

The Hopi Indians, who are believed to be the oldest tribe in North America, compare the axis of the earth to the human spine: "Along this axis were several vibratory centers which echoed the primordial sound of life throughout the universe…" (*The Book of the Hopi* by Frank Waters).

During the late 1800s, Alice Bailey and the early British Theosophists traveled to India and returned to write about the chakras, bringing a greater understanding of this ancient knowledge to the West.

WHAT ARE THE CHAKRAS?

If you go to a New Age Expo or Psychic Fair or look at the classified ads in one of the Personal Transformation newspapers, you are likely to find a wide array of healing modalities including chakra cleansing, chakra balancing, and vibrational healing.

You may well wonder, *What are they talking about?* Since there is no American or International Association of Chakra Healers, there is no standardization of these terms, and those who use them may just be following their own whims. But after you have read this book, you will at least be in a better position to speculate about what they might mean. The best policy is to ask practitioners to describe their work to you.

There is a remarkable correlation among those who see and/or feel the chakras. Throughout various cultures, there is an agreement about the nature and function of the chakras, but there is variation in their precise number, color, and other details.

The word *chakra* (pronounced *shock-ra* or *chock-ra*) means wheel or disk in Sanskrit. A chakra is an invisible (to the normal human eye) center of spinning energy. Through the chakras, we are able to receive and transmit social, sexual, and spiritual energy. The chakras have been described as spinning vortexes, or as the multi-petalled lotus flower. These flowers, which are considered sacred in India, symbolize the path of development from a primitive being to the full evolution of unfolded awareness. They float upon the water, yet they have their roots in the mud, just as the flower of your crown chakra connects to the heavens and your base chakra has its roots in the earth.

Some psychics describe the chakras from the tailbone to the crown of the head as having progressively more and more segments or petals. However, the sixth chakra at the center of the brow is depicted as having only two petals, which may have something to do with your ability to understand the dual nature of the Universe. When you recognize both the male and female within yourself, you become whole. Out of this knowledge comes the merging with All That Is, symbolized so appropriately by the "Thousand-Petalled Lotus" of the crown chakra.

Some systems describe five, others six, some seven, twelve, or even thirty chakras. Some see them only along the spine, and others find them at the joints, at the hands and feet, and beyond the physical body at progressively higher points above the head. Some people experience the energy of the chakras at the front of the spine and others at the rear and some at both front and rear.

Some old pictures depict the chakras as wheels of light located on or close to the spine. In some pictures, each chakra is shown extending out a few inches from the front or the back of the body on a stem that opens into a round flower.

Whether you think of the chakras as wheels, spirals, or flowers, it is important to remember that they are energy systems which do not have physical form. Attempting to describe such a system is like trying to describe a sound; each person who hears it will explain it in different terms and use different analogies. There may be a variety of opinions about where the sound comes from, and disagreement about whether it is pleasant or unpleasant. Yet everyone is in agreement that it *does* exist, energetically.

Any illustration of the chakras is merely a visual aid to the imagination, not a literal physical reality. Yet some individuals are so wedded to their particular perceptions that they will insist that their perception—and theirs alone—is the true reality. Then, of course, there are still many individuals who will categorically deny the existence of anything that they cannot see with their own eyes and hear with their own ears. Back in 1927, C. W. Leadbeater wrote in his classic book, *The Chakras*, "I know that there are still men in the world who are so far behind the times as to deny the existence of such powers, just as there are still villagers who have never seen a railway train."

For the sake of simplicity, I will limit my discussion to the seven master chakras along the spine. It is easy to see how one might reduce the number of chakras from seven to six or to five, since the functions of the first and second as well as the sixth and seventh are similar.

There are differing theories about which colors (or sounds or crystals) should be used at which chakras. Since we are dealing with energy, there is an inevitable degree of subjectivity. If three people watch the same sunset, one may describe it as salmon-colored, another as pink, and yet another as red. A fourth, whom we label color-blind, may have an entirely different perspective.

In this book, I will focus primarily on the rainbow system, with seven chakras from red to violet. I will list specific colors, sounds, crystals, aromas, color-charged waters and other colored liquids that can be used to stimulate or sedate the energy at each chakra.

LOCATIONS AND FUNCTIONS OF THE CHAKRAS

Here are the locations of the seven chakras, and the primary characteristics of each one:

first chakra (base chakra) at the tailbone—The energy at this center is governed by whether you received unconditional love and affection as a child. When your first chakra is strong, you will be grounded and comfortable in your body, the world will feel like your home, and you will be competent at handling practical affairs.

second chakra, below the navel—This relates to sexuality, sociability, friendliness, and desire, not just sexual desire, but the desire for anything—friends, love, material possessions, power, God. The energy at this chakra fires up those desires and gives you the enthusiasm to reach out to achieve your goals. It is also the center of physical strength.

third chakra at the solar plexus, above the navel—This is the center of your special gift, your inner sun, and how it shines out in the world. All the digestive organs (except the large intestine) are located here, so it governs the digestion. It also relates to self-esteem and self-worth. This is the center of gut-level intuition.

fourth chakra (heart) at the center of the chest—This chakra governs your ability to give and receive unconditional love and affection. When you experience loss, your heart will remain open if you allow yourself to feel all your emotions, including both sorrow and anger. But if you try to protect yourself from pain by putting up walls, your heart energy will close down.

fifth chakra (throat) at the base of the neck—This is your center of communication, creativity, and opening to spirituality. Speech and singing originate from here. Writing and teaching are also associated with this chakra.

sixth chakra (third eye) at the center of the forehead—This is about your openness to metaphysical knowledge. It relates to your higher intuition, from which all things are known.

seventh chakra (crown) at the top of the head—From here you feel your openness to Spirit. When it is open you will experience a fullness in your meditations.

The chakras are non-physical energy centers which are located in the etheric body that surrounds the physical body.

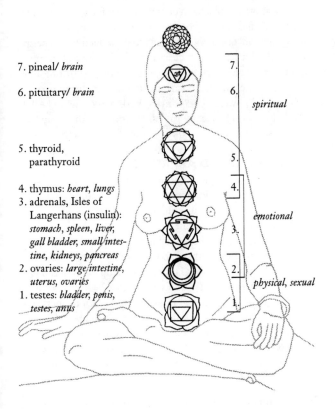

7. pineal/ *brain*

6. pituitary/ *brain*

7.

6.

spiritual

5. thyroid,
   parathyroid

5.

4. thymus: *heart, lungs*

4.

3. adrenals, Isles of
   Langerhans (insulin):
   *stomach, spleen, liver,
   gall bladder, small intestine, kidneys, pancreas*

3.

emotional

2. ovaries: *large intestine,
   uterus, ovaries*

2.

1. testes: *bladder, penis,
   testes, anus*

1.

physical, sexual

They work as energy transforming stations, enabling us to absorb energy from the environment and from other people, and transmute it into a form of nourishment for our own body/emotions/mind/spirit. When we are out of balance due to fear, stress, guilt, or confusion, our ability to draw upon these energy centers diminishes. As we clear away the blocks and become balanced and clear, we become direct conduits for ongoing streams of energies from various sources which can give us phenomenal powers. The primary work of the energy healer is to help clients to clear away obstructions so that they can have easy access to these powerful transforming stations.

AN INTEGRATED APPROACH

Chakra Evaluation, as described in the last section of this book, provides a broad picture of the health and balance of each of the chakras. Your reactions to life challenges cause your chakras to open up or close down at the physical, emotional, intellectual, and spiritual levels. Two or three chakras relate to each of these areas, so this method of evaluating an individual's health reaches far beyond a simple physical diagnosis. Once we obtain this information, we have an excellent tool for analyzing the total human being. Various methods can be used to bring the whole person into balance and health when we understand the following interrelationships:

- **Body**—The energies of the first and second chakras are associated with sexuality and with a sense of grounding, physical connections, and the desire for and ability to attract material goods.
- **Emotions**—The energies of the second, third, and fourth chakras are associated with the emotions.
- **Mind, Intuition**—The energies of the third and sixth chakras are associated with intelligence and intuition. Women's intuition or hunches come from the third chakra. The third also relates

to one's intellect and ability to retain factual information. Scientists and mathematicians have highly developed third chakras. The sixth chakra relates to higher intelligence, which is a link to higher intuition. Someone with a highly developed sixth chakra has the ability to access the Akashic Records, the cosmic library where all things are known. In ancient cultures, a man like Pythagoras might be a brilliant architect, mathematician, and also an accomplished musician, poet, and philosopher.

- **Spirit**—The energies of the fourth, fifth, sixth, and seventh chakras are associated with spirituality. At the fourth, a person may have an experience of Cosmic Consciousness, a sense of being at one with all and everything. This is a heart-opening experience which triggers deep compassion. At the fifth chakra, a person goes through the bottleneck into a new world, embracing the things of spirit, leaving behind old, narrow ways of thinking. At the sixth chakra, a person opens to a higher level of intuition and inner guidance. At the seventh, the person feels a sense of merging with Spirit.

Methods of Chakra Evaluation will be given later in the book, beginning on page 102.

CHAKRAS AND RELATIONSHIPS

We have five sensory receptors: sight, sound, touch, taste, and smell. Through each, we give and receive a vast array of sensations. Through the eyes, we receive information, and we also project our soul through our eyes to other people. Sound is a sensation that we receive and also something that we can create. Touch can be given or received. Odors and tastes can be observed and they can be produced.

Similarly, the chakras are transmitting and receiving centers where energy can be both received from other people and sent out toward other people. Let's look at some examples.

- A new mother planned her pregnancy, rehearsed the childbirth with the father, and has been waiting eagerly for the birth of her baby. Finally she gazes into her newborn's eyes, her heart chakra pulsates, and the lotus flower of her heart opens wide. The infant's heart chakra pulsates in resonance with his mother's love as he beams back a receptive enthusiasm. If this child continues to feel loved, he is likely to become a highly productive human being, with a strong sense of self-confidence (first and third chakras) and an ability to give and receive love (fourth chakra).

- A music teacher who loves his work finds that a particular student has extraordinary talent. He encourages her and takes great pleasure in her progress. This inspires her to want to perform well, and so both individuals experience an enhancement of third chakra energy, which relates to manifesting one's inner gift. The teacher's gift is to catalyze the student's natural talents and the student's gift is to express herself. In this case, there is also an enhancement of fourth chakra heart energy for both student and teacher.

- A young woman of nineteen becomes unexpectedly pregnant and is pressured to keep her baby. She eats mostly junk food and goes into labor prematurely. The labor is painful and she asks to be sedated. When she regains consciousness, her baby is in an incubator. She cannot help feeling hostile as she looks upon her infant who she feels has robbed her of her life's dreams. Her heart closes down (fourth chakra) as her power to control her own destiny (third chakra) feels defeated.

    The infant responds to his mother's vibrations with a similar resonance. Feeling unwanted and rejected, his heart closes down. Since he is dependent upon her for survival, the sense of fear this creates causes his lungs to contract, leading to an outbreak of asthma. His first chakra, which is about survival, closes down. When he grows up, he seeks drugs to numb his pain and then he steals to feed his habit. He takes unnecessary risks because he feels basically worthless and self-destructive (third chakra). He spends the rest of his life in and out of prison.

- A music teacher has failed as a musician. He resents his job and is highly critical of his most talented students (diminished third chakra). One student is particularly sensitive (open third and fourth chakras) and she tries hard to satisfy this demanding teacher. But in response to his continuous abuse, her third chakra withdraws and she feels less confident about her abilities.

Though most of us are not consciously aware of it, we also interact with our environment. The first two chakras pull up energy from the earth, soil, and rocks. The third chakra absorbs energy from the sun. The fourth chakra gains energy from the grass, trees, flowers, birds, and animals. The fifth and sixth chakras draw upon the energies of the Ancestors, the Spirit Guides, the Fairies, Masters, and Angels. Those who are imbalanced at the fifth and sixth chakras may be susceptible to negative astral influences. The seventh functions like a battery charger, renewing our connection with Spirit.

We also radiate energy to our environment. The rocks seem to enjoy being in the presence of respectful human beings. Birds and animals do love to be spoken to and acknowledged, and they are fully capable of responding to and returning affection. The grass and trees are also responsive to loving, caring energies, and the flowers will reward you with big, richly colored blooms. Beings on other planes are eager to communicate with you, if you are willing to be receptive to them. Even the sun, the wind, and the rain will respond to you when you learn to speak their language—as any Shaman can tell you.

A person who is balanced and radiant at all their chakras will be a great blessing to everyone around them—with the exception of those who are so closed down that they can only respond with jealousy and resentment. If you are nurturing the tender buds of your own opening chakras, it is often necessary to withdraw gently from such negative people until your chakras have opened into full flower and you have developed a strong sense of self-worth. This can be particularly challenging when such people are members of your own family.

If the latter is the case, it is worthwhile to explore your past-life connections with these individuals in order to see what lessons may be learned by your interactions with them. When you feel strong enough (but not before), healing these painful relationships to the best of your ability may be the greatest, most satisfying challenge of your lifetime. Often these are people who have never received unconditional love and have became hardened, convinced that they did not need love. You may be the one person in the world whom they would accept love from—if you can just find the way in.

But if you have tried with all your heart and soul, and met only with rejection, then it is time to let go and move on with your life. Do not blame yourself for their inability to receive the love that you offer.

Development of the Chakras

Let's look at the development of the chakras throughout the prenatal period, infancy, childhood, and adolescence. What causes the chakras to open or to close? Are you born with all your chakras open? As you read this section, take note of possible problem areas for yourself or your loved ones. Once you have identified problem areas, the rest of the book will give you tools for strengthening weak chakras.

KARMA AND REINCARNATION

The first chakra is strongly influenced by the circumstances of your birth and early childhood. The linear thinking of Western culture teaches us that our parents and our health are products of mere chance and coincidence. We are told that we have this one lifetime and none other in which to achieve eternal happiness in Heaven or be condemned to eternal damnation in Hell.

Eastern religions teach that the soul goes on indefinitely in a continuous spiral and that each lifetime is a rung in that spiral, offering a fresh opportunity to learn another set of lessons on the stage of material existence. Karma means that "as you reap, so shall you sow." It may take lifetimes, but eventually, whatever you do to others shall be done unto you. It is believed that karma plays a primary role in the selection of your parents, your prenatal period, and the health of your body, particularly during your early years.

Examples of Karmic consequences can be seen among those born with severe physical problems. A Vietnamese couple came to this country just as the war was ending, when she was seven months pregnant. Two months later, her baby boy was born severely jaundiced. The doctors saved his life by draining his blood and infusing his tiny body with new blood. In my meditation I asked, "Why must this child suffer such torture?"

I was shown that the baby had been an American pilot who cold-bloodedly bombed Vietnamese villages, killing hundreds of women and children. Now he was a Vietnamese infant, tortured by the Americans, and this was purging him of a huge karmic debt. Presumably the pilot died, he felt extreme remorse for his actions, and he contracted for this karmic payment. The baby grew up to be a considerate, thoughtful young man.

OPENING AND CLOSING OF THE CHAKRAS

The Spirit usually enters the body while the baby is in the womb. Newborns who experience a loving, natural birth tend to be unarmored, energetic, and completely in tune with All That Is. But even in the womb, babies who feel unwanted begin to close down their energy centers.

The chakras tend to close from the top downward. Most people close the top three chakras by the time they are three years old, as a reaction to parental and social disbelief in nature spirits, spirit friends, and in past lives. During the teenage years, the heart chakra often closes because of pain and rejection from parents, peers, and lovers. The third chakra tends to close when parents and society force teenagers into molds that don't fit. By the time they enter adulthood, most people close down all but the first two chakras. The closure of a chakra doesn't ordinarily occur in response to a single event; rather it's the repetition of similar events without relief that eventually leads to the closing of the chakra.

After high school, there is often less pressure to conform. Some young people begin to reverse the process and start opening their chakras. Usually the third chakra opens before the fourth, and all the chakras open in succession going upward. But that isn't always true. For example, people who were spiritually developed in past lives don't need to work on their higher chakras to become whole; they need to work on their lower chakras.

In reality, the concept of open or closed chakras is an oversimplification. According to Swami K. M. Tayumanavar, there are seven stages of openness for each chakra, and all the chakras are at least slightly open (the first one-seventh). So when I speak about a chakra being closed or open, these are relative terms. The seven degrees of openness are described on page 104.

The first chakra is governed by whether you received unconditional love and affection during the first three years of your life and prenatally. Did your parents want you? Did your father or mother want a boy and you turned out to be a girl—or vice versa? Did your parents speak to you when you were in the womb, and stroke your mama's belly and sing to you? When you were born, was your mama awake and excited to see you, or was she given drugs which made you groggy? Were you gently cleaned and then placed in your mama's arms to be suckled? Or were you slapped on the butt, handled roughly, and taken away from your mother? Were you able to gaze into the eyes of loving parents, family, and friends, or were you handled by doctors and nurses who didn't really care much about you?

When the circumstances of your mother's pregnancy and birth are loving, then you are likely to have a strong first chakra. If you received unconditional love and affection from your parents and/or grandparents, you will enjoy being in your body, so it will be easy for you to get grounded. Even a faithful dog can give you a sense of being loved. Some children find real comfort in companions or fairies who are invisible to the grown-ups.

If you did not receive love and affection as a child, you may develop excessive energy at the first chakra, constantly demanding attention and trying to fill your emptiness with material possessions. Or you may have deficient energy at the first chakra and feel ineffectual, unable to take an interest in life.

The second chakra holds the energy of sexuality, sociability, friendliness, and desire. The emotions are expressed through the second, third, and fourth chakras. A man's sexual organs are located primarily in the first chakra, which is about physical energy. A woman's sexual organs—the uterus, tubes, and ovaries—are located primarily in her second chakra, so female sexuality tends to be emotional. The development of your second chakra will be influenced by your parents' relationships with other people and by their attitude about sexuality.

Even in the womb, a fetus will touch its genitals. This is quite common in infants and small children. The way your parents respond to such innocent gestures will put its mark upon your ability to feel comfortable with your genitals. Your parents' feelings when they change your diapers can make a significant imprint on you. During adolescence, your parents' reaction to your interest in sexuality will make its mark on your subconscious.

Very few people are blessed with a healthy attitude toward their own bodies and their own sexuality. Very few people have a satisfying love life or sex life. A shocking percentage of women and some men were forced into sexual activity when they were children and unable to defend themselves or to make a conscious choice. Many women and some men were raped as adults. It is extremely difficult for most people to release the wounding that accompanies these experiences. Far too many people move into a permanent attitude of being victims. The work of Carolyn Myss has been effective in helping people to move out of this emotional prison.

The second chakra is also about desire. We tend to associate this word with the desire for sex, but desire is a fuel which enables you to reach out for what you want in life and draw it toward you. The desire center is at the second chakra, so people who are sexually potent are often adept at achieving a wide variety of desires. This is not to be confused with people who are obsessed with sexuality, who use their sexual energies to manipulate other people (an example of excessive second chakra energy).

People who are raised with a healthy attitude toward sexuality will enjoy their own bodies and they will be able to have fulfilling sexual and emotional relationships without controlling or manipulating their partners. A person who was sexually repressed may react by having deficient second chakra energy, being insecure, self-conscious, guilt-ridden, and subtly demanding. A person who rebels against sexual repression may have excessive sexual energy, wear rings in various body parts, take a liking to chains, and revel in sado-masochism.

Third chakra. There are two basic approaches to child-rearing. One is that children are wild, like weeds, and need to be controlled and pruned and set in the proper direction, for their own sake and for the good of society. This approach is characterized by clichés such as "Children are to be seen and not heard," or "Idle hands are the Devil's workplace."

There is another approach to child-rearing, which regards an infant like the bud of an unknown flower; that sees the parents as custodians of this new life and looks with curiosity and appreciation upon the unfolding of that child. In this second approach, parents watch carefully for signs of who this child might become.

Some societies will not name their children until the child has distinguished him or herself by some act which shows special talents or abilities. I know a woman who grew up in a family of gypsies. When she was five years old, her mother took her to a ramshackle house at the far edge of a small town, to visit an uncle. The old man told the girl to run out into the field behind the house to gather leaves and flowers.

The child came back clutching a bouquet. The wizened old man carefully placed each plant upon the kitchen table. "You see," he said to her mother, "they are all red." He pointed with his gnarled finger to three of the plants. "These ones are poisonous." He shook his head. "She will never be a healer. She must watch her temper. But she will be a fine card-reader." At the age of nine, the girl started reading cards. Because of the uncle's advice, her mother encouraged her. When she became an adult, people traveled great distances to receive readings from her. The energy at her third chakra was balanced.

We should follow our deepest desires. If we follow a path that others have laid out for us, we will always carry a sense of frustration, and when we die, we will feel that our lives were wasted. If parents and teachers understood this, they could be of great help to their children. A child who has a love of music should be asked which instrument she or he is attracted to. A music teacher should find out which music the child wants to play. If a child adores tricycles and later on bicycles and wants to take them apart, give that child the tools and some supervision to do it. Let that child spend time with a friendly mechanic. If a child adores looking at the stars, take that child to an observatory, get star maps, buy a telescope. Children know what they like, and their choices will give you clues about who they will become. If children are given the proper materials, encouragement, and support, they will develop their own natural skills, and by following their desires they will find their life's work, which will be deeply fulfilling to them. This is the most rewarding investment you can possibly make—the finest gift you can give to your children.

Kids who are forced into molds that don't fit may become resentful and rebellious against authority. When the normal channels of expression are blocked, the energy becomes excessive and explosive. Sadly, those in authority believe it is their job to break the spirits of the young, like wild horses. Yet the spirit is the essence of the third chakra, and once it is broken into submission, it is difficult to regain that sense of youthful enthusiasm.

People whose spirits have been broken will have deficient energy at the third chakra, which may include depression, lack of energy, and lack of self-worth. If such people want to find their inner source of power, they may have to go through a period of one or several years of doing nothing in particular, even watching a lot of television. Prozac is not the answer. They may need to give themselves permission to follow their whims and fancies until they find something that gives them deep pleasure and fulfillment. It may help to remember what they liked to do as children. Unfortunately, there is no guarantee that that which gives them deep pleasure and fulfillment will also bring a decent income.

Another aspect of the third chakra is the ego. It is sad that in our society when people feel openly good about themselves and about the work they do they are often labeled "egotistic." People who are spiritual are not supposed to have a strong ego. I take exception to this idea. Your ego is the face you show to the world. You do not have to be self-effacing to have a strong connection with spirit (seventh chakra). I think the confusion occurs because people who have a strong ego often become so attached to their outer personae and the accumulation of material wealth that they have no time for spiritual quests. Yet there are examples of wealthy and successful individuals who are also spiritually evolved.

Fourth chakra. Before adolescence, the same factors which influence the openness of the first chakra will also affect the fourth. When a child enters adolescence, there is a tendency to develop attachments to people of the opposite (or the same) sex. This is the beginning of "falling in love." How the object of one's affections responds or fails to respond will have an influence on one's sense of self-worth (third chakra) and the openness of one's heart. A heart that never dares to risk (probably because of past-life trauma) will tend to remain closed. This is one form of a deficient fourth chakra.

When love is experienced and returned, the heart spreads its wings and flies. The eyes open wide and the spirit soars (sixth chakra). One feels so very good about oneself (third chakra).

But if the beloved returns one's affections, and then later turns away, the shock to the heart can be enormous. The wounding to the sense of self-worth is profound. Even the spirit feels betrayed.

A similar shock can occur when the beloved moves away or, even worse, dies. How the heart adapts, or fails to adapt, to these traumas will govern the relative openness of the heart chakra.

The healthiest response to emotional loss is to grieve fully. When people allow themselves to feel the depth of their pain and to express their anger as well as their tears, they will eventually reach a place of acceptance and the ability to go on with their lives (balanced fourth chakra). Those who do not allow themselves to grieve build walls in front of their hearts. "I never want to feel that much pain again." But after a while they feel lonely, and they don't know how to escape from their own prison. These are the people who have deficient heart chakras.

Many people say, "I've cried and cried, but it doesn't do any good!" When asked, "Have you allowed yourself to feel your anger?" they will admit that they have not. Other people say, "I've yelled at my wife and broken bottles, but I still feel so angry!" When asked, "Have you allowed yourself to cry?" they will admit that crying is very difficult. The heart is a feeling place, and it cannot open fully when some feelings are allowed and others are not. If you can allow yourself to feel your tears *and* your rage, you can remove the walls.

But it may not be advisable to go back into the world with your heart wide open. The world is a dangerous place. Your heart *does* need protection. The pupil of the eye is a perfect model for protection. When you feel safe, this tiny diaphragm opens wide, becoming a window to the soul. But no one goes around that way all the time unless they are on drugs! Without even thinking about it, the pupil has the ability to shut down or open up in response to how safe it feels. When you are just getting to know someone, this aperture opens a moderate amount. As your trust grows, the pupil opens more and more. If great love is felt, it expands broadly. Yet it is capable of clamping down at a moment's notice.

Visualize a gateway in front of your heart that functions like the pupil of the eye, allowing you to respond to the circumstances of the moment by closing down and protecting your heart when that feels appropriate, or by opening up and being vulnerable. A three-dimensional version of the pupil can be seen in the sea anemone, which has tentacles like a small octopus. These colorful tentacles radiate out from a central area, like the colorful iris that surrounds the pupil. If anything threatens the sea anemone, these tentacles instantly fold in, and not a bit of color can be seen. As the threat subsides, the sea anemone opens its tentacles just a little, then a bit more, then even further, until you begin to see the color, and the tentacles gradually spread out again.

When you feel safe, the tentacles of the sea anemone spread open, and they are very attractive indeed. But as soon as you feel threatened, they can enfold your heart in those tentacles and you can feel safe.

Unfortunately, when a person feels unloved, they also tend to feel unlovable. Such a person would have deficient heart chakra energy and would be fearful and shy. Another person who feels unloved may become demanding and hyperactive. This individual would have excessive heart chakra energy and would be likely to suffer from extreme emotional swings.

Fifth chakra. This is the center of communication and creativity. It is an opening to spirituality. When a person has a transcendent experience, he or she can choose to ignore it, or it can become a stepping stone to a richer life, enabling the higher chakras to absorb more energy from the cosmos so that all of the chakras shine more brightly. This is why so many spiritual paths require devotees to fast or to dance until they go into trance or to push the outer limits of the body's endurance deliberately until the spirit apparently pops out of the body (transcends) and the person is flung into a different perspective which is distinctly beyond the limits of the individual ego (third chakra).

When transcendence occurs, the heart opens wide (fourth chakra) and a person may become surprisingly articulate (fifth chakra). One's sexual (first and second) and power (third) centers also tend to glow more brightly (unless a person deliberately closes down that energy), and a person may find that he or she is writing, lecturing, or singing with a new zest which other people find irresistibly attractive—even charismatic (fifth).

The foundation of an open or closed fifth chakra begins in childhood, when your parents either encourage or repress the expression of your thoughts and feelings. When you felt hurt or angry, were you told, "You shouldn't feel that way"? Were you encouraged to think for yourself and to speak out, or were you told, "Children should be seen and not heard!"

If you were upset, were you allowed to cry or to scream (even into a pillow)? Or were you told that "Little boys don't cry" or "Don't cry, it will upset your mother"? Were you expected to hold in your emotions like everyone else in the family, except when your mother became hysterical or your father went on a drunken tirade?

What about writing, painting, or drawing? Were these acceptable activities or were you made to feel that you were wasting your time when you should be doing chores? If you were absorbed in a creative project, did your family respect your privacy or did they come crashing in on you? If you said you wanted to be an artist, were you persuaded to become an architect—even if you had no interest in architecture?

When you entered school, did your teachers encourage you to find your own source and method of creativity or were you forced to conform to the current fashion about how to draw, paint, or write? A teacher who recognizes students' talents and encourages and mentors students can be a tremendous help in giving children confidence in their own creative process (balanced third and fifth chakras). On the other hand, parents, teachers, and peers may criticize a child harshly and dampen his or her enthusiasm for creativity, resulting in deficient energy at the third and fifth chakras.

And what about singing? Did you grow up in a family that liked to sing around the piano, or in the car? Or did people in your family regard singing as being only for professionals? When you went to school, were you encouraged to sing, or did you feel inadequate because you couldn't follow the notes or someone else had a more beautiful voice? These are the kinds of experiences that contribute to deficient energy at the fifth chakra.

A person who was forced to repress his or her thoughts and feelings may accumulate resentment and excessive energy at the fifth chakra, eventually becoming dogmatic and pedantic, insisting that everyone do things *their* way. Sad to say, this is a common profile for people in positions of authority in schools, churches, and government positions.

Sixth chakra. This reflects your openness to metaphysical things. Were you raised in an environment which regarded clairvoyance (the ability to see things like auras with the inner eye and to see into the future), clairaudience (the ability to receive Guidance and to hear voices in other dimensions), and clairsentience (the ability to feel energies) as being peculiar or crazy, or belonging to the devil? Were you taught to distrust telepathy (the ability to read minds) and telekinesis (the ability to move objects with the mind)? All of these circumstances will lead to an imbalance of the sixth chakra. This certainly describes the vast majority of human beings on the planet today.

Or were you raised among people who had paranormal abilities who encouraged and supported you in exploring your own? As a child, did you have invisible companions? Did you see fairies and elves? Did you see ghosts? Children who do not have emotional armoring, and who have not been programmed about what is and is not acceptable, often have the ability to see beings on other planes (an aspect of clairvoyance). Some children have complete recall of their past lives, or of the time spent in the womb.

When children reveal these things to their parents or other adults, the reaction of these authorities will influence whether they will feel good or bad about their experiences. If they are told, "Don't ever talk about that again!" it is likely that they will close down and feel guilty about what they have experienced and the sixth chakra will retract. On the other hand, if an adult is understanding and open-minded about the possibility that the child may be telling the truth, this helps the child trust her or his own experience. This child is more likely to grow up to be intuitively discriminating, with a balanced sixth chakra.

When the third eye is shut down, people lose faith in their own perceptions and it is easier to control and manipulate them. It is not surprising that modern society discourages mastery of the higher chakras. People who think for themselves are a threat to authoritarian governments and religions. So the modern world has produced a healthy share of notorious megalomaniacs who have excessive energy at the sixth chakra, who want to conquer and control the world.

Seventh chakra. I used to believe that all religions and spiritual paths led to the same goal. It was just a matter of personal preference which path you happened to choose.

Then a man came to me who suffered from severe migraine headaches. There was precious little energy at his sixth and seventh chakras. When I took his personal history, he told me that he was raised as an orthodox Hasidic Jew in New York City. He was sent to a private school and was required to wear black clothes and a black hat and to let his sideburns grow long. Instead of playing with the other children on the street, he was kept indoors, reciting endless doctrines. Understandably, such harsh discipline imposed on a young boy led to a deep resentment toward religion, and his higher chakras closed down.

As one Catholic man remarked, "If opening the crown chakra means opening to spirituality, I don't want to have anything to do with it!" When he had been a child, his mother tied his hands to the sides of his bed at night so he wouldn't "soil himself." She skimped and saved to send him to a private Catholic school where the nuns taught him that his body was filthy. His crown chakra energy was predictably deficient.

Over the years I found that when the crown chakra is closed, this is usually the byproduct of a repressive religious upbringing, in which a person thinks of God as a cruel, punishing, repressive father figure. There is no joy, no love, no sense of unity and compassion associated with this deity. Instead, the followers of such religions are taught that their bodies are evil, that women are dangerous, that sexuality (other than for reproduction) leads to damnation.

Yet I have met Catholic priests and Jewish rabbis and leaders of other organized religions who were kind and loving and who brought great comfort to their congregations. These were people who promoted unity among their followers, and who encouraged their followers to have their own personal experience of Spirit.

If you are a member of an organized religion, you can do a simple test to inform yourself about the nature of that group. Just ask yourself honestly, "Does this group promote and encourage unity or divisiveness? Do they say that theirs is the only path to salvation, or do they acknowledge other paths? Do they promote guilt and shame and make the body and sexuality sinful, or do they encourage people to become comfortable in their bodies? Do they create a strong dichotomy between good and evil, or do they encourage people to find a middle ground and to be compassionate? Do they associate women with evil and consider them less spiritual than men, or do they see women as equal with men?"

Many people who have open crown chakras have had a profound spiritual experience in which their usual sense of being separate and apart falls away and there is a feeling of being at One with All and Everything. There is a profound sense of merging. There is a sensation of Unity that allows one to identify with the rocks, the trees, the flowers, the birds, the animals, the whales, the dolphins, the ocean, and with other human beings. The sense of compassion and love is overwhelming. There is, in essence, a feeling that All of This Is God, and I Am a part of all of this so I, too, Am God.

It is possible to be open at the crown chakra and still be divided between body and spirit. There are many spiritual paths that promote the opening of the higher chakras while closing down the lower ones. When this is based upon voluntary celibacy and a conscious desire to transmute and channel the energy of the lower chakras into the higher ones, it is a perfectly acceptable choice. Ideally, guilt, shame, and sin will not be a part of these religions, and those who walk these paths will not stand in judgment against those who choose other methods of spiritual expression.

Overview of Chakra Correlations

The following seven chapters describe each chakra in terms of its ancient names and symbol, location on the body, and the various healing modalities that can be used to influence it. This chapter gives descriptions of the categories that will be used to discuss each of the seven chakras.

People who have inner vision can actually see or feel the chakras. You may be able to do this yourself: lie on your back and hold your hand a few inches above your body, moving from the pubic area to the top of your head. You may feel the chakras as intense concentrations of energy, and you may see the colors of the chakras with your third eye, even if you aren't looking directly at them (it may be easier to do this with your eyes closed). You can also try to see the colors of a friend's chakras.

The first three centers are below the chest: these are called the lower chakras. The heart chakra at the chest and the top three centers are called the higher chakras (though sometimes this term is reserved just for the top two or three chakras).

The assignment of different illnesses, ailments, and emotions to particular chakras is also somewhat artificial. In fact, there is (and should be) a great deal of flow between the chakras; it's only our minds that need to put things into categories.

Some authorities believe that as people raise their consciousness, the higher chakras open and the lower chakras close. I envision higher consciousness as an opening of all the chakras.

My Spirit Guide, Dr. Laing, says, "In a highly evolved person, the chakras are like progressively larger fountains, with the yellow of personal power tumbling over the orange of sexuality, which is brimming over the small but brilliant red of a firm foundation."

NAMES

These are the most common names for the chakras, beginning with the ancient Sanskrit names (and their translations).

SYMBOL

According to Hindu tradition, each chakra has a symbol. I've given simple versions of these symbols. Each chakra is shown within a circle surrounded by lotus petals. The circle represents the spinning vortex of energy, and the lotus petals represent the segments like those of an orange, that some psychics describe at the chakras, and also the gradual awakening of the whole self, finally culminating in the fully opened lotus at the seventh chakra.

My interpretations are a combination of my research and my own intuition.

LOCATION

There are differences of opinion about the location of the chakras, but when you consider how ancient this knowledge is and how many cultures it spans, there's a remarkable degree of agreement. The chakras are simply spinning whorls of energy which interpenetrate the body. The epicenter can be felt or seen two to three inches beyond the body, in both the back and the front. I've given the locations where I feel the greatest spin of energy, and this corresponds to the areas where most people currently describe feeling the energies.

AREA OF THE FACE

The face is a microcosm of the body. The same colors, aromas, and crystals that are used to treat the seven chakras can be used to treat the seven areas of the face.

SENSE

Each chakra corresponds to a different sense such as smell, taste, and touch. (*Please note:* I have changed some of the areas of the face and the corresponding Senses since writing *Color and Crystals.*)

COLOR AND ANTIDOTE

Each chakra has a particular color. Various systems assign different colors to the chakras. I've used the rainbow system beginning with red at the first chakra and ending with violet at the seventh.

An antidote counteracts the effect of a substance, as hot antidotes cold and cold antidotes hot. The colors and characteristics of the three lower chakras can be antidoted by those of the three upper chakras, and vice versa. The center (heart) chakra is balanced and needs no antidote. These are the antidotes for the colors of the chakras:

> Red antidotes blue and blue antidotes red. (Red is the color of the first chakra and blue is the first above the heart.)
>
> Orange antidotes indigo and indigo antidotes orange. (Orange is the color of the second chakra and indigo is the second above the heart.)
>
> Yellow antidotes violet and violet antidotes yellow. (Yellow is the color of the third chakra and violet is the third above the heart.)

This concept is essential in color healing, as can be seen in this statement from Dr. Laing: "If a baby's skin is too red, then it is overly excited. This condition should be watched closely, because it can become habitual and lead to red conditions such as heart troubles and high blood pressure in later life. If the baby's mother learns to handle it in early life, these patterns can be changed."

Dr. Laing advises, "Help the baby to relax. To do this, help the mother to relax. Impress upon her that her relaxation is good for the baby. Give her plenty of blue light. Put her under a blue lamp. Have her wear blue clothes. Listen to soothing music. Bring in blue flowers. Create a soothing environment."

When a person has characteristics of excess at a particular chakra, this may be treated by the antidote and the vibratory tools associated with the chakra that corresponds to that color. In the above example, the baby's skin is too red and he is highly excitable. These are characteristics of excess at the first chakra, which calls for the antidote, which is the color blue and all of the vibratory tools associated with the fifth chakra. He could be held under a blue light, or dressed in blue clothes. He could be massaged with oil to which a little blue chamomile oil was added for calming, or a few drops of blue chamomile oil could be added to his bath to relieve tension and anxiety. While she bathed him, his mother could tone to him, using the u (as in blue) sound.

TONE AND NOTE

Each chakra vibrates at a different frequency or vibration and on a different note. When you chant the tone on the given note, this may vibrate the chakra, awakening and opening it. If you find that you can achieve the same effect by using a different tone and note, feel free to use it.

ELEMENT

Each chakra corresponds with one of the elements such as earth, air, fire, and water.

CRYSTALS

When used for healing, crystals are placed on the body, in the general vicinity of the chakras, though any crystal may be used at any part of the body. Healing stones can also be placed around the body, to create an electromagnetic grid. They are also used as jewelry, though most people are unaware of the vibrational influence of the stones they wear. When you understand the healing power of stones, you can deliberately wear them in the vicinity of the chakra which will most benefit, and you can avoid wearing jewelry that would be counterproductive.

I have categorized the crystals according to the chakras where they are most commonly used. The color of the crystal often corresponds to the color of the chakra, as red stones are used at the first chakra. However, black and brown stones are also associated with the first chakra because it relates to the earth, and these are earth colors. As a general guideline, the rough stones help bring up buried, rough emotions, while the smooth stones are used to calm and soothe the nerves.

Here are some definitions that may be helpful. Technically the word *crystal* is defined as a solidified substance which has a regularly repeating arrangement of atoms resulting in natural external plane facets. By contrast, a *rock* refers to a large piece of stony material, and a *stone* refers to any earthy or mineral matter. *Quartz* is a term for minerals composed of silicon dioxide, which have six external plane facets leading to a single point (a point is a *termination*). The quartz family includes clear quartz (also referred to as *crystals*), milky quartz, amethyst, rose quartz, smoky quartz, and citrine. *Gems* are cut and polished stones, and *jewels* are valuable gems that have been prepared to be used in jewelry. Jewels and gems are usually *translucent*, which means that you can see light through them.

Organizing the crystals according to the chakras is the perfect way to get an overview of crystal healing. By going from the macrocosm of the rainbow to the microcosm of colored crystals, we have a perfect model for understanding color and crystal healing. Red and orange are earth colors. Thus the red and orange stones are good for connecting with earth energies. We think of the sun as yellow, and we call the nerve plexus which is located at the area of the third chakra the "solar plexus." When we lie in the sun we relax and expand and tend to feel good about life and about ourselves. The third chakra relates to your personal power; your inner sun and how it shines out in the world. Yellow stones are good for radiant relaxation, happiness, and strengthening the will power. Turquoise is a third chakra stone because it is intermixed with copper, which is yellow.

The fourth chakra relates to the color green in the rainbow, and also to pink. Green is nature's way of loving us. We breathe better in the presence of trees, and the chest is at the fourth chakra. Pink and green stones are most popular for healing the heart and lungs. Pink flowers have always been associated with love. Pink stones relate to unconditional love and the feminine mother energy. Green stones relate to protective love and the masculine father energy.

The fifth color of the rainbow is blue, which is the color of the sky. We think of going up into the heavens when we open to our spirituality. Blue stones help you to relax and to go into that meditative alpha state. They are used at the throat chakra to help remove anxiety so you can communicate more effectively. They help you to get in touch with the muse of creativity, which is like a special kind of spirit guide.

The sixth color is indigo, a purplish blue color, like sunset in the mountains. The purple stones like sugilite help to strengthen your spiritual energies. The seventh color is violet, like amethyst, which helps to transmute energies, like day turning to night. I also think of diamonds and clear quartz in relation to the crown chakra, like the stars and the snowflakes, each one totally unique, helping you to transcend or to gain insight in a variety of ways.

After using the crystals for healing, it is beneficial to cleanse them in some way. The clear quartz crystals particularly absorb energies. There are many methods for cleansing and renewing the energies of the stones. I like to hold them under cold running water for 10 to 30 seconds. Energy follows water, and this enables any negative energy that may have gotten attached to the stones to go down the drain, where they can be absorbed by the earth.

AROMAS

The most common way to use aromas in healing is through the application of essential oils, which are subtle, volatile liquids distilled from plants. These oils can be added to massage oil, or to your bath, or they can also be diffused into the room in a diffuser or various other devices that can be plugged into an electrical socket or even the cigarette lighter in your car. The aromas that arise from these oils can also be released by simply crushing a plant between your fingers, tossing a dried plant on a fire, smoking it like a cigarette, cigar, or moxa (used in Chinese medicine), or burning it as incense. Or you may just want to sit next to a flowering plant which exudes your favorite aroma.

The aromas may be categorized according to the chakras. One method is to observe the color of the flowers that the aromatic oils are taken from; another method is to take note of which parts of the body are most strongly influenced by the aroma of the plant. Please consult an aromatherapist or a good book on aromatherapy for more information on how to use aromatic oils.

STATEMENT

The succinct phrases in this category were received during meditation when I asked my own chakras to speak and describe themselves to me. I've found that on different days (and for different people) they respond differently. These "statements" can be used as loose (and sometimes amusing) guidelines. Try it yourself.

EXPLANATION

In this category I describe the essential energy of the chakra, often quoting from my Spirit Guide, Dr. Laing, and *The Book of Guidance*, which I channeled.

BALANCED, EXCESSIVE, AND DEFICIENT ENERGY

If a child is confronted with aggressive behavior, he or she may respond by becoming aggressive or by assuming a superior attitude. These are expressions of excessive energy. On the other hand, if a child encounters indifference, she or he may respond by becoming depressed or lethargic. These are expressions of deficient energy. People with either deficient or excessive energy are imbalanced in their chakras. This is not unusual. Rather, the balanced individual is unusual in our society.

When your childhood and adolescence have been healthy and you feel well-nurtured, you may be balanced and open in every chakra. But when there is unreleased emotion such as fear or anger accumulated from years of past experience, and when there has been a lack of love and encouragement during the developmental period, the energy flows less freely to these centers. This may result in either excessive or deficient energy at the chakras, depending upon the personality and the kind of rejection or negative experiences that person has had. This is best explained in the chapter on the Development of the Chakras.

In each chakra chapter I have given the main characteristics of that chakra and examples of three types of individuals who have dominant personality traits in each of these chakras. These individuals represent the balanced, excessive, and deficient personality types.

Many of the examples of personality types may sound like stereotypes, but they are all descriptions of actual people. The sexes and the professions can be reversed. Not all of the characteristics need apply.

You may get a mixture of excessive and deficient characteristics in one person, or an individual may swing back and forth between excessive and deficient, sometimes passing through a temporary balance. When the energy of a chakra is clearly deficient, it should be treated with the corresponding color or other vibratory tools (sound, aromas, food, etc.) of that chakra. However, if the energy is excessive, it can be treated with the antidote for that chakra (the antidotes are given on page 34).

For example, sexual energy comes mostly from the second chakra which is orange, so someone with excessive sexual energy may benefit from the antidote, which is indigo. This color and the vibratory tools associated with the sixth chakra will calm the sexual energy, making the person feel less compulsive. An alternate treatment is to use yellow, which strengthens the third chakra, putting the person more in touch with his or her personal gift, which in turn enhances feelings of self-worth, making this person less desperate for sexual satisfaction.

The personality will usually reflect either the energy of the highest open chakra or the chakra with the most energy and focus. For example, I imagine that Mozart may have been a balanced second chakra personality, because while his third, fourth, and fifth chakras were certainly open, he seems to have enjoyed focusing much of his energy through his second chakra. As Laing says, "When an evolved and balanced person focuses energies through a lower chakra, the color of that chakra will glimmer in their aura, in a particularly crystalline hue."

Under the balanced personalities of each chakra, I've mentioned various religions. I have not tried to designate religions for those who are out of balance, nor have I attempted to mention every religion.

These categories are to be taken very loosely. The same religion may be practiced by people who are focused at different chakras. For example, I placed Judaism at the third chakra, because of the Jewish devotion to The Law and The Word and because of the great love that Jews have for good food. However, there is a high form of Hasidic Judaism that is full of ecstatic song and dance, which is a fourth or seventh chakra experience, depending on who practices it or how intense the ecstasy becomes.

Similarly, I put American Indian religions at the first chakra, because of their deep connection with the earth, but there are Shamans (medicine people) who express their spirituality through the sixth or seventh chakras.

When sexuality is described for a person who is balanced, this is the expression of someone who may also be open at higher chakras but their main focus is through that chakra. When I describe the sexuality of a person who is out of balance, I am referring to the person who is open at that chakra but not necessarily at the higher chakras.

CONTRAINDICATIONS
People who have the listed symptoms should not use the color of that chakra.

GLANDS AND ORGANS
INFLUENCED BY THE CHAKRA
Each chakra will have an influence over the endocrine glands and internal organs that are located in the area of that chakra. Sometimes the influence will cover a broader sphere, as happens with the first chakra, which is located at the tailbone and which rules not only the bladder, vagina, and male reproductive organs but also the blood and spine.

ILLNESSES AND AILMENTS
The illnesses and ailments that are given will tend to respond well to treatment with the color and other vibratory tools which correspond to that chakra. Methods for healing the chakras will be explained briefly in the final chapter.

First Chakra

Names
Muladhara (Support)
Kundalini Center
Root Chakra
Base Chakra

Symbol
The symbol for the first chakra is a square (yantra), symbolizing the earth, the foundation. Within the square is a downward pointing triangle, the symbol for female sexuality. Within the triangle is a linga, the symbol for male sexuality. A snake, the symbol for the kundalini, coils three-and-a-half times around the linga. On the outside are four lotus petals.

Location
at the tailbone

Area of the Face
chin, jaw, lips

Sense
touch—as experienced by the multitude of nerve endings on the lips

Color and Antidote
red
Antidote, blue

Tone and Note

Tone, e (as in red)

Note, c

Element

earth

Crystals

The first two chakras relate to the earth. In some creation myths, the Creator forms the four races of human beings from the four colors of the earth. Red, orange, brown, and black are considered earth colors. The orange stones are reserved for the second chakra, but the red, brown, and black stones are all used at the first chakra. Red stones are used for energy and blood circulation. Brown and black stones are used for grounding (connecting with the earth, with your body, and with physical reality). When using crystals at the first chakra, two stones are used; one at each groin point, where the thigh joins the torso. When worn on the body, first chakra stones may be placed in hip pockets.

Red Garnet. Has an arousing, invigorating energy. Good for enthusiasm and self-confidence. Place on lower back for menstrual cramps or low back pains. Red ruby can be used instead. (Caution: many people become overstimulated by red stones, especially when worn above the waist.)

Black Obsidian. Excellent for grounding, for people who are too spacey. If you've been running around all day and you need to get centered, or if you've been doing intensive inner healing and you don't feel stable enough to drive your car, hold a large piece of obsidian in your lap for a few minutes. Black onyx has similar properties. (Caution: do not use black or brown stones at your heart chakra unless you want to close down your emotions.)

Aromas

Aromas which have aphrodisiac properties are associated with the first and second chakras. For the first chakra I list the musky animalistic odors (which are not enjoyed by all) and for the second, the more subtle ones. Also for the first chakra are the aromas which promote a sense of grounding.

Patchouli. A thick dark yellowish-brown oil with a greenish tinge, patchouli is musty and pungent and—for those who like its distinctive odor—it has an aphrodisiac appeal. Can be used as a perfume. It is a stimulant and antidepressant that is commonly used in China, Japan, and Malaysia. It is useful for cracked skin and athlete's foot (the feet are also associated with the first chakra).

Geranium and particularly Rose Geranium is light green and vaguely resembles the odor of rose oil. You can use it as a perfume, placing a few drops behind your ears. It stimulates the adrenal cortex, which governs the balance of hormones, including male and female sex hormones. It is helpful for premenstrual tension and for menopause. It is also used for fluid retention, which often occurs premenstrually.

Statement

"I want stuff."

Explanation

The first chakra concerns your connection with the earth, your birthplace, your culture, your foundations. The first chakra is influenced by your earliest relationships. If there was one person (or even a dog or fairy godmother) who gave you unconditional love, you're likely to have a strong first chakra, and your survival mechanism will be good. If you didn't receive unconditional love, your first chakra may be weak, unless you have done considerable healing of your inner child.

This is the center of physical energy and vitality. It's grounded in material reality, so it is the center of manifestation. When you're trying to make things happen in the material world, in relation to business or material possessions, the energy to succeed will come from the first chakra.

Red, the color of passion, is used to arouse attention and interest. A woman who wants to be noticed should have a pair of red high heels. Passion is a source of power and self-confidence. It is an intensity of energy and even anger. It is the source of great strength, which will help you to move through challenging situations.

Sometimes anger which is repressed erupts as fever or inflammation, all of which are excessive red conditions.

Balanced Energy at First Chakra
Characteristics
centered
grounded
self-mastery
healthy
fully alive
unlimited physical energy
can manifest abundance
able to express anger without doing harm
spiritual expression could be
  Celtic
  Shamanism

Hatha Yoga
Hawaiian Kahuna
sexual energy:
affectionate
able to trust and be vulnerable
sensuality is felt throughout the body

Example
This Native American Indian medicine woman and midwife expresses her spirituality through seasonal rituals which involve specific places in nature, use of herbs, dancing, and chanting. Her eyes sparkle and though she is in her seventies she walks and laughs like a young woman. She has plenty of energy and always knows what to do.

Excessive Chakra Energy
Characteristics
egotistic
domineering
greedy
addicted to wealth
sexual energy:
indiscriminate
focus is entirely genital
nervous sexual energy
may be sadistic

Example
This wealthy perfectionist is the owner of a California restaurant chain. He rules his employees like a demanding general. He is nervous and chronically constipated. He owns

three cars. He sleeps with many women, but he "can't get no satisfaction."

Deficient Chakra Energy
Characteristics
lacks confidence
feels spacey and unfocused
weak
can't achieve goals
self-destructive, suicidal
sexual energy:
    feels unlovable
    fears being abandoned
    little interest in sex
    masochistic

Example
This unskilled, insecure woman lives in a chaotic house and spends most of her time watching television. Her parents were alcoholic. She's underweight and often forgets to eat. She's chronically depressed, has no energy, and little interest in men. Life holds no pleasure for her.

Contraindications
Avoid red for all nervous and red conditions including
agitation
hyperactivity
fever
ulcers
high blood pressure

red face

swellings

inflammation

epilepsy

Caution: If you use red light on the head, limit the treatment to three minutes and apply a cool wet cloth or a blue cloth to the head during the treatment or for at least two minutes afterwards. Red is the most potent color, and the easiest to overdose with. If you feel nervous, angry, hot, or uneasy while sitting under this light, discontinue it. Sit under the blue light for a few minutes as an antidote.

Glands and Organs Influenced by the First Chakra

blood

spine

nervous system

bladder

male reproductive organs

testes

vagina

Illnesses and Ailments to be Treated with Red

Since red is the antidote for blue, it will be used to treat blue conditions. Since it's stimulating, it will be used to treat slow and weak conditions. Since it's in the first chakra area, it will be used to treat organs which are located in the lower region of the body. Since it is red, it can be used to cleanse and build up the blood. Red is used for the following conditions:

depressed, fearful

debilitated, lack of energy

spaced out, ungrounded

low blood pressure
bladder infections
sluggish digestion
inactive, flaky skin
shock
anemia
poor circulation
impotence, frigidity
infertility
no menstrual period
after childbirth, if weak (or if there's been much blood loss)
menopause, if weak (alternate with longer doses of blue if there are hot flashes or a feeling of agitation)

Second Chakra

Names

Svadisthana (Abode of the Vital Force)

Sacral Center

Splenic Chakra

Symbol

The crescent moon symbolizes receptivity and the womb. It is the symbol of femininity. On the outside are six lotus petals.

Location

1–2 inches below navel or branching to left side of spleen

Most people have a concentration of orange energy an inch or two below the navel. But for some people (particularly those who have chosen to be celibate) this chakra will branch off to the left side of the body and settle under the left rib cage at the spleen, which is why this is sometimes called the splenic chakra. Then it will have a blue-green color.

Area of Face

mouth, gums, tongue, cheeks

Sense

taste (both the second and third chakras relate to the sense of taste)

Color and Antidote

orange (below navel)

blue-green (at spleen)

(See notes under Location, above)

Antidote, indigo

Tone and Note

Tone, o (as in home)

Note, d

Element

water

Crystals

Orange stones are used for the second chakra. The tiger's eye has a soft feminine energy and the carnelian has a strong masculine energy.

Tiger's Eye. Soothes away worries and apprehensions, especially anxieties about love and sex. If you are feeling the pains of love, this stone will remind you that you can change your energy and make it smooth. Tiger's eye makes a good gift between lovers; enhances telepathic communication.

Carnelian. This is the stone of worldly success. It will give you the courage to project yourself with warm self-confidence. Carnelian promotes self-esteem and enhances sexual energy.

Aromas

The aromatic oils which are used for the first and second chakras are fairly interchangeable. If you're looking for an oil to use as an aphrodisiac, be sure that the aroma is pleasing to both parties.

Jasmine. This is a dark, viscous oil which has a heavy, almost animal quality. The white flowers must be gathered at night, since that is when the aroma is strongest. High quality oil is very expensive, but only a tiny amount is needed. Massage on the abdomen and lower back during childbirth to relieve pain and strengthen contractions. It is also used for post-natal depression. Jasmine strengthens the male sex organs and will reduce an enlarged prostate. Its aphrodisiac properties are helpful with both impotence and frigidity.

Sandalwood. The sandalwood is a small evergreen parasitic tree that grows in India and Australia. The oil is yellowish to deep brown and is extremely thick and viscous. It is a powerful urinary antiseptic, used to treat various infections of the urinary tract, and was formerly used for gonorrhea. Used for oily skin and acne as well as dry skin, it is excellent in aftershave lotions for barber's itch (the cheeks correspond to the second chakra). It is also an effective aphrodisiac.

Statement

"I desire" (This could relate to money, sex, God, or anything else.)

Explanation

The second chakra is about friendliness, creativity, sexuality, emotions, and intuition. It governs people's sense of self-worth, their confidence in their own creativity, and their ability to relate to others in an open and friendly way. It is influenced by how emotions were expressed or repressed in your family during your childhood.

Orange is a sociable color since it combines the physical red with the intellectual yellow, so it's good to use in living rooms and family rooms, classrooms, and social areas in hospitals. I prefer a light orange because reddish orange can be overstimulating, which can lead to nervousness. Red-orange is a great color for parties.

It's rumored that the reason why one popular fast-food chain has bright orange and pink seats is because the pink attracts customers, and the orange is friendly but keeps the customers energized so they don't want to relax and stay too long.

The second chakra is one of the centers of the emotions and it is in the area of the large intestines. Consequently, when you feel emotionally imbalanced, you're likely to experience diarrhea or constipation.

The second chakra is the center of physical prowess. In Chinese martial arts, it is called the *tan t'ien* and in Japan it is the *hara*. Students are taught to run their energy through this area, which is located 2 to 3 inches below the navel.

The second chakra is the sexual center particularly for women, because the uterus, fallopian tubes, and ovaries are located here. This may be one reason why women tend to be more emotional about sexual relations. When the second chakra has a healthy spin, it indicates that this person has a healthy sex life or at least a healthy attitude toward sex. *The Book of Guidance* says, "Fill your sexual organs with radiant acceptance. Feel your sexual desires finding union with your spiritual desires.

"Herein lies the Mystery of Mysteries, Desire itself is the Divine Motivator. Sexual energy is required to fire all other energy...

"The orange energy gives you the ability to reach out, to radiate, to extend yourself. It gives you the forcefulness to reach *up*—to your heart, and to your soul.

"Regard your sexual center as a precious fountainhead of vital energy. Explore that energy, learn to channel it, and eventually you will learn to use it as a part of your Total Self, to achieve whatever goal you seek…"

The second and fifth chakras are both related to creativity. The womb is at the second chakra, so it is a cradle of creativity, the center of gestation. Creative energy requires freedom and resists constraints, so this can lead to rebelliousness or an unwillingness to be controlled and an intolerance for authoritarianism.

Balanced Chakra Energy
Characteristics

friendly, optimistic

concerned for others

has a sense of belonging

creative, imaginative

intuitive

attuned to one's feelings

gutsy sense of humor

clairsentient: can merge with the body and mind of another person and psyche them out in order to better understand them

may have vague memories of out-of-body experiences such as flying

spiritual expression could be

Pentecostal

Osho style yoga

sexual energy:

extremely sensual

highest goal is to have a wonderful orgasm

may desire children

Example

Mozart (as portrayed in the movie, *Amadeus*) is a delightful example of a man who has a well-developed second chakra. He is friendly, jovial, self-confident, courageous, and outrageous. He actively pursues his own creativity. He writes raucous, unconventional, "immoral" operas and falls in love with a beautiful, sexy young woman whom he marries despite the fact that she is beneath his class.

Excessive Chakra Energy
Characteristics

emotionally explosive

aggressive

overly ambitious

manipulative

caught up in delusion

overindulgent

self-serving

clairsentient (see above), but can't distinguish between one's own feelings and the feelings of other people

Sexual energy:

obsessed with thoughts of sex

sees people of the opposite sex exclusively as sex objects

requires frequent sexual gratification

Example

This woman works as a fashion model and sells cosmetics on the side. She is obsessed with her appearance and spends most of her money on clothes, jewelry, and perfumes. She values herself according to how much attention she receives from men. She is constantly looking at men's bodies and comparing them to her ideal of the perfect male. She uses men to get what she wants and when she feels rejected, she blows up.

Deficient Chakra Energy
Characteristics
extremely shy, timid
immobilized by fear
overly sensitive
self-negating
resentful
buries emotions
burdened by guilt
distrustful
sexual energy:
> clinging
> feels guilty about sex
> has difficulty conceiving
> feels abused
> frigid or impotent

Example
This fellow is shy and retiring, gentle and thoughtful. Secretly he thinks that sex is crude and often suffers from impotence.

Contraindications
excessive energy
excessive sexual energy

Glands and Organs Influenced by the Second Chakra

skin

mammary glands (milk produced through ovarian hormones)

female reproductive organs

kidneys

Illnesses and Ailments to be Treated with Orange

kidney weakness

constipation

muscle cramps and spasms

insufficient lactation

lack of energy

allergies (hypersensitive to environment)

repression and inhibition

Third Chakra

Names
Manipuraka (Jewel of the Navel)
Lumbar Center
Solar Plexus Center

Symbol
The triangle is pointing down, with swastika marks on the three sides. This is the fire wheel. This chakra is associated with the sun and the ego. It is also the center of digestion, which the Chinese call the triple warmer because heat is generated in the process of digestion. On the outside are ten lotus petals.

Location
at the solar plexus (below the breastbone, behind the stomach) or at the navel

Area of the Face
throat (which leads to the stomach and small intestines)

Sense
taste (in common with the second chakra)

Color and Antidote
yellow
Antidote, violet

Tone and Note

a-o-m (ahh-oo-mmm)

Note, e

Element

fire

Crystals

Third chakra healing stones are usually yellow. Turquoise is included here, because it contains copper which has a yellowish color, and because it is beneficial for the digestive organs, which are located in the area of the third chakra.

Citrine. Helps you to relax and feel good about yourself. Allows you to get in touch with your personal power and to express your unique gift. Strengthens the will power and improves self-esteem. Useful for those who want to break a drug habit. Aids digestion and frees up your breathing. Yellow topaz has similar properties.

Turquoise. This is a stone of peace, harmony, and beauty, in perfect attunement with Spirit. It is good for those who are afraid of power, or who need to use power in a balanced way. Beneficial for digestive problems when worn near the third chakra. Increases your vibratory and healing powers, and enhances inner wisdom.

Aromas

In addition to the digestive organs, the nerves and the mind are also associated with the third chakra. These aromatic oils and teas are excellent for calming the nerves, soothing the digestion and stimulating the mind.

Peppermint. Used as an aromatic oil in candy and various medications, this herb is famous for settling the stomach and (as a byproduct) freshening the breath. Remember that the throat corresponds to the third chakra. Has a beneficial effect on the stomach, liver, and intestines. Massage the stomach with oil to which a few drops of peppermint has been added as an antispasmodic for colic, indigestion, vomiting, and stomach flu.

Lemon. Lemon oil relieves anxiety and depression and combats fatigue and lack of energy. Add a few drops to warm massage oil and apply to the back in light, gentle strokes. Use in a diffuser for stimulating the memory and for mental alertness. To relieve vomiting, put a couple drops on a tissue and inhale. For diarrhea, put a few drops in massage oil and gently massage the lower abdomen and lower back, then inhale from the hands with several slow deep breaths.

Statement

"I want happiness."

Explanation

The third chakra is the center of personal power. When the third chakra is open, you have found your own unique gift, the work that gives you pleasure and makes you feel fulfilled. When you're at the third chakra level of development, it's appropriate to build a positive self-image (ego). At the sixth chakra level you'll need to let go of your attachment to that image.

One way to find your gift is to consider what you most enjoyed doing when you were a child. This will give you clues about your natural inclinations. It's quite a joy to discover that what you're supposed to do is what you most deeply desire to do.

Your gift will reflect your natural skills and aptitudes, but it will also respond to training and schooling. For example, an opera singer is born with a beautiful voice but requires training to develop that skill. Dr. Laing says of people who are balanced at their third chakra, "Their personal will aligns with the Cosmic Will. These people are on their own path developing their intelligence and personal power, making unique contributions in the world."

According to Paramahansa Yogananda this chakra is ruled by the conscious mind. It is active only while awake. However, it can be trained in introspective, creative thinking which will then provide access to and influence on the subconscious mind. This helps to explain the power of negative or positive thinking.

In the martial arts the third chakra is considered the center of chi, the life force energy. So this chakra relates to physical abilities and athletic prowess.

This is the center of gut-level intuition. "I just knew it was going to rain," and "I had a feeling you were going to call," are statements that typify the third chakra intuition. (There's another kind of intuition that's found at the sixth chakra.

Yellow is the color of happiness. As an example of how this works, when I was living in Seattle I was involved in an unhappy relationship when a psychic woman told me that I needed more yellow. One gloomy day, I had a terrible argument with this man, and I stomped out of the house and walked up the street.

As I was walking, I saw a whole rock face covered with beautiful yellow and orange flowers and I said to myself, "She said I need more yellow," so I proceeded to inhale the rich colors of the flowers. Within minutes I was filled with joy.

After that I painted my desk yellow. I liked it so well that I painted my bookcase yellow. That was so pleasing that I painted my whole room yellow.

The Book of Guidance says, "You see my sun as yellow.

Through the color yellow I give you warmth and an inner glow. I radiate. This is the source of relaxation. Deep relaxation. Because you relax when you feel accepted. Then you can stop trying so hard. When you come out to the beach and lie in the sun, you relax completely because you know that nothing is expected of you. When you know that nothing is expected of you, you can just relax and be yourself. Now there is a place at the center of your body called the solar plexus. Just as my sun radiates acceptance, warmth, and relaxation from the center of your universe, you can also radiate acceptance, warmth, and relaxation from the center of your being."

Dr. Laing says, "Yellow goes straight to the soul. It is the common man. Common as the daisy and the dandelion. This soul is accessible to everyone. It is not esoteric or occult; it is ordinary.

"It [yellow] is the Middle Way. The Controller and Regulator. The Center of Strength. It is our link with the great Central Sun. It receives the radiations of the heavens and sends tentacles down to earth. It is a source of heat and energy without overstimulation. Nourishing like sunlight."

When parents have specific goals for their children, this sets up a conflict in the child's will. The child will be torn between love for the parents, and the need to develop his or her own power. If the child is loyal to the parents' expectations, he or she will probably not find his or her own unique form of creative expression. This is how people develop what appears to be a superiority complex. The superior attitude comes as a reflection of parental pride in this person's achievements. But secretly, this person feels inferior because he or she never had an opportunity to develop a true sense of self-worth.

Dr. Laing explains that in a less developed person, yellow will be mixed with red, indicating an obsession with accumulating things for one's self. Personal power will be directed in a self-serving direction and will not bring with it a sense of fulfillment.

"The third chakra relates to digestion," explains Laing. "A balance of energy here causes good digestion. A lack of energy here leads to poor digestion. Yellow relates to relaxation at meals and the flow of juices; digestive juices and bile, as well as adrenal and sexual hormones, all things that flow and radiate. Not blood because that is red and of the first chakra. But it does control dilation and constriction of the blood vessels.

"Since the third chakra rules both the digestion and the mind, it is difficult to think when too full or too hungry. But fasting will calm the mind unless there's a disorder here. Radiant relaxation comes from here. The solar plexus is the Center of Breath."

The diaphragm is located at the third chakra, so the color yellow at the third chakra is helpful for someone who is not breathing deeply because of tension or fear.

Balanced Chakra Energy
Characteristics

outgoing

cheerful

has respect for self and others

has a strong sense of personal power

in touch with one's gift

skillful

intelligent

relaxed

spontaneous

expressive

takes on new challenges

enjoys physical activity

enjoys good food

may have vague feelings of astral influences, both friendly and hostile

spiritual expression could be

    Jewish

    Karma Yoga

    Tharavada Buddhism

sexual energy:

    cares about one's partner

    highest goal may be to have a simultaneous orgasm

    sense of responsibility toward mate and children

    uninhibited

    relaxed

    can show emotional warmth

Example

This man owns a large health food store and restaurant. He loves to cook and rarely uses a recipe, preferring to cook spontaneously. He derives great satisfaction from his work, and he creates a pleasant environment since he is friendly to both his employees and his customers. He's self-disciplined, reliable, and flexible.

Excessive Chakra Energy
Characteristics

judgmental

workaholic

perfectionistic

overly intellectual

as employer: very demanding

as employee: resents authority

may need drugs to relax

superiority complex fluctuates with hidden inferiority complex

Sexual energy:

　　demanding

　　constantly testing one's partner

　　complains a lot about the relationship

　　can be very affectionate

　　may desire a lot of sexual activity, but rarely feels fulfilled

Example

This fellow is very talented, but cannot decide how to channel his energy. He's a science teacher, carpenter, and musician. His father was a physicist and encouraged him to choose a career in science. He's a good science teacher. He drives himself very hard, but he doesn't enjoy his work. He complains frequently about his life, his job, and his co-workers. He worries about money constantly, and makes long lists of how he'll spend it when he gets it. He has many fantasies about women, but when he's in a relationship he's critical and argumentative. He has a pot belly and indigestion.

Deficient Chakra Energy
Characteristics

depressed

lacks confidence

worries about what others will think

confused

feels controlled by others

poor digestion

afraid of being alone

sexual energy:

    insecure

    needs constant reassurance

    jealous, distrustful

Example

This man is usually unemployed, though he's a skillful welder. He feels overwhelmed by life and can't seem to accomplish anything. He spends a lot of time smoking marijuana and hangs out at the local bar with his friends, most of whom also have deficient third chakras. His wife is a competent woman who supports him and tries to boost his ego. He's possessive of her and may become violent if he thinks she's interested in someone else. Yet he has affairs whenever he pleases.

Contraindications

People with nervous conditions and hot, red conditions should limit their use of yellow light to about ten minutes.

Glands and Organs Influenced by the Third Chakra

the diaphragm (and the breath)

adrenals

skin

digestive organs: stomach, duodenum, pancreas, gallbladder, liver

Illnesses and Ailments to be Treated with Yellow

digestive difficulties

gas

food allergies
liver problems
diabetes
hypoglycemia
over-sexed
hypothyroid
gallstones
muscle cramps, spasms
mental and nervous exhaustion
depression
difficulty breathing

Fourth Chakra

Names
Anahatha (Unbeaten)
Heart Center
Dorsal Center

Symbol
Two triangles, one pointing up and the other down, representing balance. The heart is the center, with three chakras above and three below. The six-pointed star, also known as the Star of David, symbolizes the awakening of spirituality while being firmly planted on the ground.

Location
center of chest

Area of the Face
nose (leading to the lungs)

Sense
smell

Color and Antidote
green or pink
Antidote, none needed, since it's central and balanced

There are two aspects of the love energy at the heart; the feminine/mother energy which we associate with pink and the masculine/father energy which we associate with green. On the rainbow, green is the color between yellow and blue. So where does pink come from? Magenta, a hot pink, is produced by combining violet (the spiritual energy of the crown chakra) with red (the grounded energy of the first chakra). A person who is balanced at their heart chakra tends to have this combination of qualities.

Tone and Note

Tone, a (as in ah)
Note, f#

The combined sounds of everything on earth compose a harmonic chord which is the keynote of our planet. It's the key of f (or f#), whose note becomes visible as green. This sound is good for quieting the mind.

Element

air

Crystals

Pink and green stones and combinations thereof are associated with the heart chakra. Pink stones hold nurturing mother-love energy and green stones are associated with protective, fatherly love.

BC Jade. When your heart feels threatened or frightened, this dark green jade from British Columbia is like a loving father, reaching out to give comfort and reassurance. It is grounding, stabilizing, and protective. The Chinese say that jade (Chinese or BC) gives wisdom, clarity, justice, courage, and modesty. It will give you the wisdom to make clear judgments, the courage to follow through on them, and it will prevent you from getting big-headed about the good results.

Rose Quartz. The gentlest of stones, this pink quartz penetrates to the heart and the brain, soothing away worries. It carries the energy of unconditional love. It is comforting for those who have been hurt in love. Rose quartz helps to heal the wounded inner child. For those who wish to stop drinking alcohol, carrying a piece about the size of a quarter can help alleviate the need for alcohol.

Watermelon Tourmaline. This beautiful pink and green stone makes you feel as if you're being held in loving arms which make you feel safe enough to let yourself be vulnerable. Watermelon tourmaline helps to open dark places that have been shut down within your heart.

Aromas

Ylang Ylang. Sometimes the flowers of this small tropical tree are pink, and sometimes mauve or yellow. The oil varies from almost colorless to a pale yellow and the aroma is extremely heavy and sweet. It is used to slow down over-rapid breathing (hyperpnea) and over-rapid heartbeat (tachycardia), and is useful in conditions of shock and anger. It is used to reduce high blood pressure. It is antidepressant, aphrodisiac, and sedative, helping to reduce the anxiety often associated with sexual performance. It helps to balance the male and female energies. Too much can cause nausea and/or headache.

Rose. This deep reddish brown or greenish-orange essential oil is not distilled, but is produced by enfleurage, which requires a huge quantity of rose petals, so the cost is very high, but only a tiny amount is required. It is a gentle but potent antidepressant and is especially comforting for those who are grieving. It is an aphrodisiac and the Romans used to scatter rose petals on the bridal bed. Rosewater has similar properties and, since it is produced by distillation, it is far less expensive.

Statement

"I want to give and receive love."

Explanation

The heart chakra is the center of compassion. When this chakra opens, you transcend the limits of your ego and identify with other people, plants, animals, and all of life. This is the humanitarian center. When your heart chakra is open, you're likely to become involved with social causes. You'll care about things like ecology and saving the whales. You may find yourself working in one of the helping professions and participating in meditations for peace.

The heart chakra is your most vulnerable place. When you're hurt in life and love, the first impulse is to close your heart and say, "I'll never let anyone do that to me again." Of course, when you build a wall around your heart, you're keeping yourself locked in. Every time you experience a loss, you'll either go through a process of grieving, feeling all your feelings (especially anger and sadness), or you'll close off your heart and remain in a state of denial, becoming numb to pain as well as pleasure.

In fact, the majority of people have closed off their hearts—often at a very young age—which accounts for the alarming amount of apathy that exists in the world today. A major part of healing is to mend the heart. Your heart is at the center of your body and when your heart energy flows, your whole being is full. Then you radiate love energy to everyone around you.

Green is the color of healing. Almost all the healing herbs are green. Since it's at the center of the spectrum, green is the most balanced color. When you feel tense, it's wonderfully relaxing to go for a drive in the country or sit in a meadow of green grass. Green is nature's way of loving you.

Pink is the most powerful color for sending love to another person. When a person feels needy, you can mentally direct a ray of pink light toward them and you'll notice an immediate change, even if they are on the other side of the world. One of my clients lived with a man who constantly fought with her. I advised her to send him pink light when he was irritable. The next time he harassed her, she sent him pink light and, to her amazement, he immediately stopped arguing.

There's a common affliction of fourth chakra people. Since most of them used to be third chakra people, they're often married to third chakra people. As their fourth chakra opens and they evolve spiritually, they no longer share the same values with their mates.

Since the male sexual organs are in the first chakra, the center of physical reality, men tend to be more physically active. This energy is readily transferred to the third chakra, which is the power center. Men adapt well to becoming third chakra achievers, though this is more difficult for women, who frequently suffer from a fear of their own power.

The female sexual organs are primarily in the second chakra, which is at the seat of the emotions. This energy is readily transferred to the fourth chakra, the center of uncon-ditional love.

The Personal Transformation Movement is basically a heart chakra phenomenon. This helps to explain why there are more than twice as many women involved in this move-ment. Many (third chakra) men feel threatened when their (fourth chakra) wives become involved in such activities. However, there can be compatibility between a person focused in their fourth chakra and a person who is focused in their third chakra, provided that both personalities are well balanced.

Balanced Chakra Energy
Characteristics
compassionate

humanitarian

balanced

sees the good in everyone

desires to nurture others

friendly, outgoing

active in the community

discriminating

in touch with feelings

empathetic—instinctively aware of the joys and sorrows of others. May feel their aches and pains

spiritual expression could be

Sufi

Unity

Bhakti Yoga

Mahayana Buddhism

sexual energy:

has the ability to surrender and merge in a love relationship

desires a oneness of body, mind, and soul—and will feel lonely in a relationship that gives less than that

strong will power, which makes it easier to wait for the right partner highest goal is to experience Divine Bliss—a spiritual, emotional, physical sensation—while in the embrace of one's beloved

Example

This Sufi teacher lives in a huge house, surrounded by luxurious, profuse flowers. She is perpetually housing, feeding, and comforting everyone from beggars to saints. Children are drawn to her. She has endless friends and overflows with energy and love. Her lover is both affectionate and spiritual.

Excessive Chakra Energy
Characteristics

demanding

overly critical

tense between the shoulder blades

possessive

moody

melodramatic

manic-depressive

uses money to control people

has the attitude of a martyr: "I've made so many sacrifices for you…"

Sexual energy:

 a master of conditional love: "I'll love you if…"

 withholds love to get the desired behavior: "you wouldn't do that if you loved me."

Example

This man is a poet and actor. He's a passionate lover, full of emotions rarely expressed except through his art. Outwardly he seems sincere and devoted, but inwardly a fire rages and he can't control his moodiness, his depressions, his grief, his fatigue. When he's alone he's miserable, and when he's newly in love, he's ecstatic. But after awhile he becomes demanding and controlling and he drives away the ones he loves.

Deficient Chakra Energy
Characteristics
feels sorry for oneself

paranoid

indecisive

afraid of

  letting go

  being free

  getting hurt

  family members getting hurt

  being abandoned

sexual energy:

  feels unworthy of love

  can't reach out

  terrified of rejection

  needs constant reassurance

Example
This is the woman who loves too much. Because she wasn't well loved as a child, she doesn't believe she's worthy of love. She may be attractive and competent, but she chooses a mate who resembles the father or mother who was unable to give her the love she craved. Her greatest desire is to change her mate into a loving person through the power of her love. She does everything for him, but she ends up trying to control him and he often resists by pushing her away.

Contraindications

Glands and Organs Influenced by the Fourth Chakra

heart

lungs

immune system

   thymus gland

   lymph glands

Illnesses and Ailments to be Treated with Green or Pink

heart pain

heart attack

high blood pressure

negativity

fatigue

difficulty breathing

tension

insomnia

anger

paranoia

cancer

Note: The best color for treating cancer is green. Ordinarily white light can be used for any ailment, because it contains all the colors. However, white light is nourishing and should not be used for cancer, because it feeds the cancer. Green is nourishing only to the healthy cells.

Fifth Chakra

Names
Visshudha (Pure)
Cervical Center
Throat Center

Symbol
The circle of unity with All That Is comes within the triangle, indicating an increasing openness to Spirit.

Location
bottom of neck

Area of the Face
ears

Sense
sound

Color and Antidote
blue
Antidote, red

Tone and Note
Tone, u (as in blue)
Note, g#

Crystals

Fifth chakra stones are blue. They influence the throat and voice box. Since they are blue, they may be used as an antidote wherever there are red conditions such as inflammation, irritation, agitation, or fever. When used as an antidote, it is best if the stone is of at least equal size to the area being treated.

Sodalite. This blue stone with streaks of white calcite soothes all ailments of the throat and eases communication. It will help you to put your thoughts and feelings into words. It is a balancer that will enable you to keep your head in the clouds and your feet on the ground. Sodalite is invaluable for travel sickness, depression, feeling too "spaced out," and bad drug experiences. It is soothing to the third eye when doing psychic work. This stone will deepen your concentration.

Azurite. This blue stone is often found in geometric clumps, or in combination with malachite, when it is called azurite-malachite. Azurite stirs up the throat chakra and penetrates the voice box so that you're filled with the desire and ability to speak. Azurite keeps you centered and articulate. Azurite-malachite is good for bringing up the emotions (malachite) and then making you want to talk about them (azurite). Use two small smooth stones of azurite or azurite-malachite over the ovaries for menstrual cramps or ovarian discomfort, or place them over strained eyes (for example, when you've been using a computer for too long).

Aromas

These oils either have blue flowers or relate to the ears.

Blue (German) Chamomile. A fine oil is produced from this daisy-like yellow and white flower (which is also good for the third chakra). Its soothing, calming, and anti-inflammatory properties are due to azulene, the active principle which appears blue in highly distilled oil. It is beneficial for reddened skin conditions. Add a few drops to a warm bath to alleviate stress or tension. It is soothing, calming, and antidepressant. For calming babies, add a few drops to massage oil or use drops diluted in oil for the bath. For earache, rub around the ear, or apply hot compresses of chamomile. There are several different types of chamomile, but they all have similar properties.

Eucalyptus. During hot days, eucalyptus trees seem to give off a blue haze. This oil is used for cooling the body. It helps reduce fevers. Eucalyptus oil may be used in a hot or cold vaporizer to ease a tight, dry cough. Used in gargles. It is anti-inflammatory. Add a few drops of this oil to massage oil to relieve muscular aches and pains. It can be found in most drugstores.

Statement

"I want to speak freely and openly."

Explanation

When you reach this level of spiritual development, you have to squeeze through a bottleneck. It's a struggle. Society doesn't require it of you—in fact, many people frown upon it. Most people function from their lower chakras and they can't understand the person who opens to spirituality. It makes them uncomfortable. If you open your fourth, that's extraordinary. But to open your fifth is like walking on thin ice.

The fifth chakra is the center of communication, so as you open this center, there is a desire to talk about your extraordinary experiences. When you do this, some of your old friends will fall away. But your true friends will always be there, so try to let go of the ones who are uncomfortable with you. New and wonderful friends will be magnetically drawn to your new persona. Fortunately, there is a growing community of people who have opened their fifth chakra.

Spiritual children are those who have not closed down their fifth chakra. Their parents allow them to speak freely, to sing, and when necessary, to cry and scream. They've been encouraged to trust their own perceptions and to follow their instincts.

These children may experience conflict when they enter school and encounter a new set of values. This often results in chronic sore throats or ear infections (which indicate an inability to speak freely or an unwillingness to hear what is being said to you). The blue light will comfort these children. They need to talk about the conflict they're feeling and be reassured that their reality—though it's different from the norm—is valid.

One of my students is a kindergarten teacher. After learning about the calming effect of blue, she instituted a new program. On days when all the kids are climbing the walls, yelling and screaming and acting out, she'll say, "Today's a blue day!" Then she'll bring out blue poster paint and blue play dough and blue construction paper and blue magic markers and she'll tell each child to do a project in blue. She says the effect is remarkably calming. In fact, blue classrooms are used for hyperactive children and blue holding rooms are used in prisons.

Blue can also be used effectively for the dying. Blue pictures, blue blankets, and blue flowers are calming and soothing to one who is letting go of life. If you're sitting by the bedside of a person who is dying, the tone "u" (as in blue) can help to calm his or her nerves and accompany that person into a different reality. Try it, and see if the effect seems beneficial. Perhaps this person will want to join you.

Balanced Chakra Energy
Characteristics
   contented

   centered

   can live in the present

   perfect sense of timing

   good speaker

   musically or artistically inspired

   can meditate and experience Divine Energy

   easy grasp of spiritual teachings

   may be overwhelmingly prolific

   clairaudient: may hear voices or celestial music from the other planes

   spiritual expression could be

   Quaker

   Spiritualist Church

   Agni Yoga

   Private worship

   sexual energy:

   when all five chakras are open, can manifest incredible sexual or sensual energy, or can abstain without great effort

   may choose to rechannel sexual energy into music, art, or meditation

   may vacillate between seeking bliss through sexual embrace and seeking bliss through celibacy and meditation

Example
This man is a popular writer, choosing unusual topics of a metaphysical nature just as the public becomes ready to read

such material. He plays the violin for pleasure. He's highly intuitive, living fully in the present, waiting until everything feels right before making any moves. He is always at the right place at the right time. He practices T'ai Chi and meditation daily. He's devoted to friends and family, though he sometimes goes off into the mountains for weeks at a time. His wife shares his interest in combining spiritual and sexual energies, and they're both sensual and uninhibited.

Excessive Chakra Energy
Characteristics
    arrogant
    self-righteous
    talks too much
    dogmatic
    addictive
    Sexual energy:
        preoccupied with sexual thoughts
        may be unconsciously macho
        prefers partners who can be dominated

Example
This therapist is a large, overbearing, bitter woman who has a lot of anger toward men. She's an articulate champion of women's rights, and has deep insights which make her a good therapist and writer. When she likes someone, she's a good friend, but when she turns against a person, she can be rude and abusive. She attracts sexual partners who are submissive and meek.

Deficient Chakra Energy
Characteristics
scared, timid
holds back
confused
quiet
inconsistent
unreliable
weak
devious, manipulative
can't express one's thoughts
sexual energy:
> can't relax
> feels conflict with religious upbringing
> afraid of sex

Example
This fifty-five-year-old woman was once a lawyer, but she dropped out in order to follow her spiritual master. Sometimes she has deep insights, feelings of ecstasy, and experiences a profound love of Spirit. At other times she feels like a failure and a misfit. She's in conflict about her sexuality. She's nervous and worries a great deal. She lives in a communal house and doesn't fit in. She's afraid to express her needs openly so others consider her devious and manipulative.

Contraindications
Do not use blue light for more than thirty minutes, or it may cause you to feel withdrawn and sleepy. If this occurs, follow the treatment with a few minutes of yellow or orange.

Do not use blue for the following ailments:

colds

muscle contractions

paralysis

poor circulation

Glands and Organs Influenced by the Fifth Chakra

throat

thyroid

nerves

eyes

muscles

Illnesses and Ailments to be Treated with Blue

Since virtually every illness is characterized by inflammation, which is a red condition, blue is the most frequently used color for healing. Use it to heal all hot, red, and nervous conditions. Use it as an antidote for irritations in the first chakra area.

hyperthyroid

sore throat

inflammations

burns

skin irritations, rashes

fever

ear infections

overtired

mentally exhausted

gum inflammation, teething

ulcers, digestive irritation

nervousness
colic
back pain
hemorrhoids
high blood pressure
toxemia of pregnancy
vaginal infections
hyperactive
excitable and violent
terminal illness

Sixth Chakra

Names

Ajna Chakra (Command)
Third Eye Center
Christ Consciousness Center

Symbol

Suddenly the multiplicity of petals falls away and you are left with two huge petals. Through letting go of your attachment to the multiple distractions of the world you enter into a Divine relationship with Spirit. This is the ego self and the spirit self, the reasoning and the intuitive minds, the pineal and the pituitary, the masculine and the feminine. All dualities converge at this point. The triangle is the yoni or female energy and within it is the linga or male energy. The linga of the first chakra was black, whereas this linga is white. The linga of the first chakra was surrounded by a snake, coiled three-and-a-half times around it, symbolizing the sleeping kundalini energy at the base of the spine. Now the kundalini energy rises to the sixth chakra; the snake uncoils and the sexual energy rises upward. The crescent moon of feminine receptivity embraces the circle above it. This circle is a golden dot which is the essence of spiritual energy. It represents being in your center. The quarter moon is an energy vortex symbolizing infinite potential.

Location

Each of the chakras can be located at the back or the front of the body, along the spine. The sixth chakra is found at the base of the skull, at the medulla oblongata. Its location at the front of the head is between the eyebrows at the third eye.

Area of the Face
eyes (the windows of the soul)

Sense
sight

Color and Antidote
Indigo (a purplish hue)

Indigo is a combination of blue and red. Red is warm, so indigo is a way of calming without cooling or slowing.

Antidote, orange

Tone and Note
mm or OM (as in home)

The sound "o" represents the sun or third eye, and "m" represents the moon or medulla. OM unifies both sides. It also combines the "o" of the second chakra with the "m" of the sixth chakra. This tone dissolves dualities and creates unity. It brings the ego self into union with the Spirit self.

Note, high "a"

Element
electrical or telepathic energy

Crystals
The crystals of the third eye are mystical stones which have powerful transformative properties.

Lapis Lazuli. This rich royal blue stone is usually streaked with iron pyrite. Use it at the third eye to take you deep within the vaults of your mind. Lapis facilitates hypnosis, visualization, astral travel, and understanding of metaphysical teachings. It brings your energies to a higher level during meditation when placed on the crown chakra. Polished lapis helps you to shed your ego and put your spiritual life first.

Sugilite (Luvulite). This rare stone has just been discovered in the last two decades. It combines the purple of the sixth chakra with the black of the first, bringing spirituality into every cell, integrating body and soul. Sugilite is ideal for highly sensitive, idealistic children, or adults who find it difficult to function in a less-than-ideal world. It reminds you that you are special and your gift is rare and valuable. It helps you to visualize how to bring your gift to the world.

Aromas

Juniper berries. Made from the ripe purple berries of the juniper bush, juniper oil helps overcome anxiety, insomnia, and mental fatigue. It is good for greasy hair and dandruff. It strengthens the kidneys and relieves fluid retention.

Rosemary. This pine-like evergreen helps to balance body and mind. It was used by the ancient Egyptians, Greeks, and Romans as a symbol of love and friendship because it clears the mind, stimulates the memory, and is good for the heart. Rosemary oil is used to relieve headaches, migraines, and fatigue. It was used in funeral wakes and at burial grounds because it purifies the air and prevents infections. It makes the hair shiny and eliminates dandruff when used in a rinse.

Statement

"I want to see clearly."

Explanation

The third eye is the center of psychic power and higher intuition. Through the sixth chakra, you can receive Guidance, channel, and tune into your Higher Self. This is the center that enables you to experience telepathy, astral travel, and past lives.

When this center is agitated, it often indicates that a person had early religious training that taught him or her to be afraid of the occult. Many cultures and religions have taboos against anything vaguely metaphysical. While it's true that so-called magical powers have been severely misused throughout history, the same can be said for any kind of power, particularly political power. And it is political power, including the political power of the established churches, that has outlawed or defamed practitioners of the occult, usually for the simple reason that these people were attracting too many of the churches' clientele.

The irrational guilt and fear created by these taboos make it difficult for most people to get a clear perspective so they can judge for themselves whether a teaching is beneficial or not. First it's useful to make a distinction between black magic and white magic. White magic harnesses natural energy for positive purposes. If you're in the presence of someone who practices white magic, you'll feel normal, or perhaps your energy will be enhanced. Black magic manipulates energy for selfish purposes. When you're in the presence of someone who uses black magic, your energy may be temporarily boosted, but within a short time you'll feel drained.

The energy of the third eye is, unfortunately, accessible to all people regardless of their moral and ethical values. The ability to manipulate reality is an appealing skill for those who are power-hungry, and this includes many New Age gurus.

So be discerning about who you accept as a spiritual teacher. If you feel at all distrustful about such a person, pay careful attention to your perceptions.

For many people the word guru has disturbing implications of blind obedience and hero worship, and this has been a damaging pattern that many followers of gurus have fallen into. But guru is just another word for spiritual teacher. If you're fortunate enough to find a spiritual teacher you can trust, who feels like an innately ethical person, and if it feels like this person has the desire to help you to experience the fullness of your being, this can be a great blessing. A true spiritual teacher should be simply a person who has progressed further in their spiritual development than you have. Ideally it will be someone who has opened their higher chakras and achieved self-realization (balanced sixth chakra). If this is your goal, then such a person can be a great help. In every field where we seek to gain knowledge, we look for a teacher who is more experienced and more knowledgeable than we are. The same should apply to the field of spiritual development.

Unfortunately, most gurus demand absolute and blind obedience. While this can be useful for a short time—to overcome attachments of the ego—when it is prolonged, it robs the devotee of his or her ability to function effectively from their own center of power (third and sixth chakras) and to be discriminating. Also it places the guru in the light of the seventh chakra, even while the guru is professing to lead the student into a deeper relationship with the Self and the Divine One.

Before the third eye opens, you see through two eyes: you experience a duality between your normal self (your conscious mind, intellect, ego) and your higher Self (your intuitive mind, or Spirit). When the third eye opens, these two images merge—like when you see a double image through the lens of a camera and then bring it into focus as a single unified image.

I don't believe in forcing yourself to shed your ego through self-denial. I believe in working with the ego until it recognizes that the fulfillment of its highest dreams is to be found through merging with the High Self and becoming One with the Divine. Then all the masks fall away: who you thought you were, who you thought you ought to be, who your parents wanted you to be. Suddenly you let go and your True Self shines forth. "I am what I am." There is no guilt, no need for illusion or pretense. You are totally in the present and you realize that you were there all along.

The pineal gland is an endocrine organ that has the essential structure of an eye. It's located in the central part of the brain, so it relates to both the sixth and the seventh chakras. It functions as a light receptor, and is believed to be responsible for ovulation occurring in response to the phases of the moon.

When the kundalini rises up the spine, it stimulates the pineal gland, which may explain the experience of seeing the Pure White Light. The third eye is the Christ consciousness center. Everyone can have Christ consciousness. Jesus said, "The light of the body is the eye: therefore when thine eye is single, thy whole body also is full of light; but when thine eye is evil, thy body also is full of darkness." *Luke* 11:34.

The yogis say that the pineal is the seat of memory, so when the kundalini rises this storehouse opens up and you become a witness to all your past lives, and you see into your future. You no longer require the veil of forgetfulness because you're no longer afraid of who you are—you have nothing to hide. You're flooded with compassion and forgiveness and unconditional love toward all of your selves in all of your lives and you see yourself in everyone and everything. You no longer have any karmic debts. You stand released from fear and guilt and when this occurs, you transcend the wheel of karma: you realize that it was only a reflection of your ego.

Thus you become a fully realized being. This is the meaning of self-realization. You merge with Spirit and you become the Spirit within yourself: you realize your full potential.

Balanced Chakra Energy
Characteristics
charismatic

access to the Source of All Knowledge

receives Guidance

experiences Cosmic Consciousness

not attached to material things

no fear of death

can show the way to liberation, through example

clairvoyant: may begin with waking visions of vague colors and landscapes

experiences telepathy, astral travel, past lives

not preoccupied with fame or fortune or worldly things

master of oneself

spiritual energy could be

    Essene Christian

    Taoist

    Vajrayana Buddhist

    Raja Yoga

sexual energy:

At this level of development, one perceives oneself as essentially androgynous, and no longer requires another person for completion. A needy partner distracts one's inner bliss. Thus celibacy is a natural choice, but not a necessary one.

Example

The Dalai Lama has conscious memory of his previous incarnations and he carries the knowledge of that lineage from birth. He is considered the incarnation of Avaloketeshvara, and it is his mission to return in human form in order to show people the way to liberation. He is kind and compassionate, a master of himself. From the time he was a young boy he demonstrated deep wisdom and remarkable abilities.

Excessive Chakra Energy
Characteristics
egomaniac
proud
manipulative
religiously dogmatic
authoritarian

Example

Ayatollah Khomeini is a dogmatic religious leader of Iran who persecuted anyone who did not agree with him. He was a fierce authoritarian and women were kept submissive and oppressed in his country.

Deficient Chakra Energy
Characteristics
non-assertive
undisciplined
oversensitive to the feelings of others

afraid of success

may be schizophrenic (unable to distinguish between ego self and Higher Self)

Example

Sometimes this schizophrenic woman believes she is Joan of Arc, and will display dynamic strength and the ability to heal by touch and to foresee future events. Then she'll sink back into a self-effacing personality, barely able to feed herself, afraid of everyone, distrustful, unable to find any direction in life.

Contraindications

schizophrenic

withdrawn

Glands and Organs Influenced by the Sixth Chakra

pineal

pituitary

brain

ears

Illnesses and Ailments to be Treated with Indigo

pain (anesthetic effects)

diarrhea

agitation and tightness in intestines

psychic exhaustion

Seventh Chakra

Names
Sahasrara
Thousand-Petaled Lotus
Crown Chakra
Wisdom Chakra

Symbol
The fully open lotus, the flower in fullest bloom, symbolizes being totally open to the Light. You've lost all individual identity and now you merge with All That Is. You become a fully realized being. This is self-realization, the peak experience of which is called samadhi.

Location
crown of head

Area of the Face
the crown of the head, including the scalp and hair

Sense
extrasensory perception (ESP), the "seventh sense"

Color and Antidote
violet

Note: gold is also associated with the crown chakra
Antidote, yellow

Tone and Note

Tone, e (as in bee)

Note, high b

Crystals

The violet-colored stones and the clear crystals which are like the stars in the sky are favored at the crown chakra.

Amethyst. This lovely violet-colored translucent quartz gives protection by allowing in only those energies that are harmonious to you and deflecting and transmuting all other energies. Use over your third eye to facilitate visualization and past life recall. Keep a cluster in your room or on your altar to calm and center your energies. Place in rooms where disharmony is felt or anticipated. If you have difficulty sleeping, hold it while you meditate before going to bed. Place a piece in wine or beer to detoxify the alcohol. Amethyst is beneficial to wear as jewelry, but not if you are nervous or hyperactive.

Clear Quartz Crystals. These hold the vibration of White Light. They absorb, transmit, resonate, and amplify energy. Crystals are good to hold while you meditate. They enhance the energy of group meditations. Placed around the home, they give off negative ions that create a sense of well-being. Be cautious about wearing clear quartz as jewelry if you aren't feeling clear, or if you're around negative people, because they can absorb negative energy and reflect it back to you. If they are kept clean, they have the ability to bring more color and light into your aura.

Aromas

Lavender. This oil is specially recommended for all ailments of the head, brain, and nerves. Several drops may be added safely to the bath water or to massage oil or used directly on the skin as perfume. Small quantities of lavender oil have been shown to calm spasms of the solar plexus. It is also excellent for insomnia, infections, allergies, fainting, headaches, migraines, influenza, insomnia, hysteria, and tension.

Frankincense. The name derives from Medieval French, meaning "Real Incense." It was the first kind of incense to be used. The essential oil comes from a resin with a somewhat camphorous penetrating aroma, familiar to Catholics, where it is used in the incense burners. This practice dates back to ancient times when it was called Holy Oil and was used by the Hebrews and Egyptians to drive out evil spirits. It has the ability to slow down and to deepen the breath, which contributes to feelings of calmness, which in turn is conducive to meditation. It is used in inhalations, massage, and bath oils for respiratory infections, chronic bronchitis, asthma, and for people who have had strokes. Steam inhalation is not recommended for asthmatics. It is believed to help those who tend to dwell too much upon their past.

Statement
"I want to be lazy." (The seventh day is the day of rest.)

Explanation
When a person enters the seventh chakra, the person you were dies. Every layer of ego attachment falls away. You die to your old self. At the fifth chakra, you may long to leave your mark for posterity. At the sixth chakra, there is no more longing; it is enough to simply be a living example.

At the seventh chakra even the desire to help falls away, though it may emerge again unpredictably. Now you become the divine madman or madwoman, utterly beyond laws and norms, totally unpredictable and unaccountable. Your behavior may be considered antisocial, amoral, and incomprehensible. But you are totally moral according to your own ethics.

You have the power to transmute matter into energy and energy into matter, which enables you to perform remarkable feats such as walking on water or appearing at several places at the same time. Food can be produced out of thin air. But then, you're not likely to want to attract much attention, being neither a martyr, a saint, nor an egotist. So you're more likely to wander around in the Himalayas if you want to be left alone, or to wander from village to village, communicating in parables.

Your spirituality is omnipresent, and since you live constantly in The Light, there's no need for a path by which to get there, so there's no need for any organized religion.

Sexuality isn't likely to be desirable to you, though you may have evolved a form of energy exchange that's quite ecstatic though it is not focused at any particular part of the body.

The seventh chakra is the point where the silver cord detaches from the body at the time of death. The silver cord is the fine line that allows us to astral travel and then return to the body. When this cord is severed, death sets in.

Death is no stranger to the seventh chakra person.

Since there is no separation between self and spirit-self, the body is a joke; a trick of the mind. Bodies come and go, but life is eternal. Since all the bodily cells can be transmuted and renewed, you're capable of immortality and you can perform miraculous healings and raise the dead.

Balanced Chakra Energy
Characteristics
open to the Divine
miracle worker

can transcend the laws of nature

total access to the unconscious and the subconscious

ability to leave and return to the body at will in full consciousness

ability to remain alert during and after death

almost immortal—or possibly immortal

Example

Babaji appeared to Yogananda and to Yogananda's teacher,
Sri Yukteswar, and to his teacher, Lahiri Mahasaya. He is
always described as the eternally youthful saint, who appears
and disappears at will. Yogananda believed that he was one
of the teachers of Jesus.

Excessive Chakra Energy
Characteristics

constant sense of frustration

unrealized power

psychotic, depressed, or manic-depressive

frequent migraine headaches

destructive

sexual expression

    sometimes passionate, sometimes distant

Example

This psychotic man imagines that he is Jesus Christ. He has
delusions of grandeur as he attempts to enlist his twelve
disciples. He actually does have the ability to see into the
future and to read minds, but his skills are sporadic and undisciplined, and he cannot distinguish between his fantasies, or
his paranoias, and reality.

Deficient Chakra Energy
Characteristics
    no spark of joy
    catatonic
    can't make decisions

Example
This young boy never seemed quite normal, even as a baby. He was withdrawn, uncommunicative, and rarely smiled. When he was four years old, the doctors said he was catatonic. He was quite intelligent, but unable to relate to other people. He was pale and thin. Though his parents tried to love him, he was unable to respond. He was lost in a world of his own.

Glands and Organs Influenced by the Seventh Chakra
    pituitary
    pineal
    nervous system
    brain

Illnesses and Ailments to be Treated with Violet
    depression
    migraine headaches
    parasites
    black eyes
    baldness, dandruff

Note: Violet is excellent for artists and high-strung, nervous people who need grounding but find red too harsh.

Chakra Evaluation
and Treatment

In some sense, everything you do (or don't do) influences your energy and your chakras. In this chapter, I will focus upon methods of healing that are specifically intended to balance the flow of energy at the chakras.

CHAKRA EVALUATION
Before you can treat the chakras, you must determine which ones are deficient or excessive. The depth of information that can be derived will be, to some degree, dependent upon the sensitivity and experience of the practitioner. I've outlined some of the methods for evaluating the chakras.

Intellectual/Intuitive
This is the method which you employed when you read the previous chapter. It is similar to the evaluation that the practitioner comes to from simply talking with the client and considering how their symptoms fall into the categories of the chakras.

Visual
Those who have the gift of clairvoyance can simply look at you and see which of the mini-suns that make up your chakras shine brightly, and which are dull, cloudy or muddy. There are other visual methods:

A **colored lamp** may be used to direct colored light to different chakras. For the purpose of chakra evaluation, only the corresponding colors should be used for each chakra (red for the first, orange for the second, etc.). If you feel comfortable sitting under a particular light, as though you could sit there for a long time without any problem (but not as if there was a craving to do so), this indicates that the chakra is balanced. On the other hand, if there is discomfort, ranging from tightness or pain in the head to a simple feeling of irritability, this indicates that the chakra is out of balance. The same applies if there is a sense of craving more of that color.

The **Color Receptivity Trainer** consists of a small box mounted on a tripod, which is positioned directly in front of the eyes, at arm's length from the client. This method was devised by Jacob Liberman, author of *Light, Medicine of the Future.* Light is projected through different-colored gels. You look at a circle of colored light about 4 inches in diameter. The CRT is engineered with a timer and flashing lights. The number of flashes per minute are gradually increased. Once again, the colors that cause you discomfort provide clues about which chakras might be out of balance.

Tactile/Energetic

You may **use the hands to feel the energy** a few inches above each chakra, while being sensitive to variations of temperature, vibration, and other subtle differences. Dorothy Krieger's Therapeutic Touch (described below) and Pranic Healing (described below) both use this method. Many body workers find that they become sensitive in this way. The tactile method may be enhanced by other tools.

A **pendulum** may be used a few inches above each chakra, to feel the relative size and shape of the electromagnetic spin of energy. Pendulums are usually made of a light, symmetrical object which dangles from a string or chain. A simple clear quartz crystal pendant works well. One method is to allow the object to swing freely, wrapping the chain around the fingers until just a few inches of chain remain. Ask the pendulum to give you its signal for a normal balanced chakra. It is liable to spin clockwise in a circular motion about the size of your open hand. Any variation on this might indicate that something is out of balance.

A **crystal** may be used to augment the vibratory energy, enabling the practitioner to feel the spin of energy a few inches above each of the chakras. My technique of Vibrational Alignment™ (described below) uses this method.

Biofeedback can provide an additional source of information. For example, a simple device which senses the temperature of the fingers can be attached to two of the fingers. When a person feels agitated or fearful, the blood circulation withdraws from the extremities, and this sensor picks up the change of temperature and registers a high-pitched sound which alerts you that some kind of discomfort is being registered. This device can be coupled with the use of the CRT or colored lamp.

MEASURING CHAKRA OPENNESS

The size of a healthy, open chakra is approximately the size of your open hand, with the diameter stretching from the tip of your thumb to the tip of your little finger. A large person with large hands has proportionately larger chakras, but the energy emanating from and received by a smaller person is not necessarily weaker, just as a small diamond is not diminished in radiance just because it is diminutive next to a large clear quartz crystal.

The radiance emanating from an open chakra can travel a great distance. In fact, a person can consciously choose to reach out with that radiance, to affect healing for a person who is far away. Physicists are now speculating that there is a form of energy that travels faster than the speed of light, which might help to explain the apparently miraculous effects of distant healing.

In 1927, C.W. Leadbeater wrote in his classic book, *The Chakras*, "When quite undeveloped they appear as small circles about two inches in diameter, glowing dully in the ordinary man, but when awakened and vivified they are seen as blazing, coruscating whirlpools, much increased in size, and resembling miniature suns."

One theory suggests that there are seven stages of openness at each chakra. I rarely have the gift of seeing the chakras, yet I can easily feel the spin of energy. I will describe what I feel at each of these seven stages, and how I interpret what I feel. Remember that this is a highly subjective experience and three different people who have the ability to feel the energy may describe these seven stages in three entirely different ways.

first stage—My arm feels fatigued as I attempt to feel the energy at this chakra because it is lifeless, weak, and only slightly open. The chakra has barely enough energy to keep the internal organs and endocrine glands functioning. With even just one chakra this deficient, if this condition persists, the person will be highly susceptible to disease and even death.

second stage—The energy here is slow and lethargic. The diameter of the circle is no larger than the first joint of the person's thumb. This chakra is functioning just above minimal level. This person has a low resistance to infection. Their will to live is not strong.

third stage—The spin of energy lacks enthusiasm. The size of the spin is no greater than a silver dollar. This chakra is functional. The energy is adequate but weak.

fourth stage—The energy spins at about the pace of the heart. The size of the spin is about the size of the palm of the person's hand. This is normal and within the range of healthy.

fifth stage—The energy spins at about the pace of the heart. The size of the spin is about the size of the palm, plus the first digit of the fingers. This chakra feels energetic and in excellent health.

sixth stage—The energy spins at about the pace of the heart. The size of the spin is about the size of the palm, plus the first two digits of the fingers. This chakra exudes radiance, dynamism, and enthusiastic energy.

seventh stage—The energy spins at about the pace of the heart. The size of the spin is that of the open hand. The energy is off the scales. This person is obviously exultant and basking in the light.

METHODS OF TREATING THE CHAKRAS

There are a wide variety of methods which help bring the chakras into balance and alignment. Once you have determined which chakras need work, any of the following modalities may be used. This list is not intended to be exhaustive, and new methods are constantly emerging.

Intellectual/Intuitive

Because the chakras are about energy, the intellect is not particularly effective for altering that energy. However, the intuition can be valuable for determining which chakras to treat, which methods to use, and for how long.

Visual/Color

When you have mastered the language of color, you will find yourself automatically applying this knowledge in your choice of clothing, jewelry, flowers, wall decorations, and every aspect of your life. Other methods of visual treatment include:

Color Breathing. You can look at a particular color or visualize it as you inhale, and imagine bringing that color into one of your chakras or internal organs. Colors may also be sent to others via the breath.

Color-Charged Water. Water may be charged by putting it in a colored glass container, or by putting a plate of colored glass against the window and setting the water in a clear glass jar in front of the color source. A few sips of this water may be taken several times a day, or it can be used externally, as a wash. The French word for water is eau, pronounced "o," so the names for the color-charged waters are rubio for red-charged water, ambero for orange and yellow, verdio for green, ceruleo for blue, and purpuro for indigo and violet.

Juices and Other Liquids. Any colored juice can be used to enhance the energy of the corresponding chakra. Colored wines, liqueurs, and beer may also be used.

Colored Lamp. This is a lamp that shines a strong light source through colored gels or sheets of colored glass to a specific area of the body.

Phototherapy. When the client becomes comfortable with a given color by way of the CRT (described above), then flashes are added, and the flash rate is gradually increased. Each eye contains 137 million photoreceptors that transform light into electrical impulses which travel to various parts of the brain which are stimulated by these impulses. Phototherapy begins by treating visual problems and then expands into the treatment of many other ailments.

Laserpuncture. This method was developed by the Russians as another method of using color for healing. Through the use of laser light, specific colored tubes are used to stimulate acupuncture points by low-energy laser beams. Some of the same principles that are used to correlate different colors for specific internal organs, for example, are used in laserpuncture.

Audio/Sound

Toning and Sounding. Toning is the sustained, vibratory vocal sounding of single tones—usually vowels—without melody, rhythm, or words. Sounding is the free-form use of sounds without any particular structure. By making vibratory sounds with your voice, you can tune up your chakras. The sounds which correlate with the chakras are given on my cassette tape, *The Healing Voice* (see Recommended Reading).

Tuning Forks. Each fork is U-shaped, with a stem at the bottom of the curve of the U. A person can hold a fork by the stem and then strike the fork against something like the bone of the knee, and this will set off a vibratory frequency. A set of seven tuning forks is used, and each fork is tuned to one of the seven notes of the scale. A simple chakra tune-up consists of striking each of the seven forks, beginning with C and holding the fork to the corresponding chakra, beginning with the first chakra.

Musical Instruments. Various instruments may be held or suspended directly above the chakras that need work. Crystal Bowls and Tibetan Bowls of varying sizes can be used to tune up the chakras, much as the tuning forks described above. Other instruments that have a profound effect upon the chakras are gongs, Tibetan bells, and the didjeridu, a long horn-like instrument originated by the Australian Aborigines.

Sound Tables. There are various massage-type tables with speakers installed, for example, at each of the seven chakra areas. Appropriate music for awakening, stimulating, or calming the chakras is piped in through each chakra section.

Aromas

Aromatherapy. Many of the volatile oils have a tendency to favor a particular internal organ or endocrine gland, and this—together with the color of the flower or the oil itself—gives us clues about which chakra will be most influenced, though all of the oils may be used at various parts of the body. See each chakra chapter for aromas that may be used in conjunction with each of the chakras. There are many ways to receive the benefits of aromatherapy, including using a diffuser, bath oil, massage oil, or incense.

Movement

There are specific exercises—both ancient and modern—which are designed to influence the health of the chakras. One of the oldest is called the Tibetan Rites and it is described in *Ancient Secrets of the Fountain of Youth*. An excellent modern book which gives movements and a vast array of other information about working with the chakras is *The Sevenfold Journey*. Once again, any movement, particularly yoga and various forms of martial arts, will have an influence upon the chakras. Martial arts are particularly useful for developing the second chakra.

Energy Healing

Pranic Healing. Prana means "to breathe forth" which refers to the life force that vitalizes the etheric body and nervous system. Prana is a Sanskrit term for vitality and magnetism. An important function of the chakras is to vitalize the dense physical body, including the endocrine glands. Pranic healing attempts to heal the physical body by directing prana to one or more of the etheric chakras, which is then believed to vitalize the corresponding organs and endocrine glands. The healer uses her/his breath to draw extra prana into their own body, and then sends that prana through their own chakras to the corresponding chakras of the client.

Therapeutic Touch. This method, developed by Dorothy Krieger, RN, uses the secondary chakras at the palms of the hands to feel the energy emanating from the body, particularly at the chakras, a couple of inches away from the physical body. Then the practitioner directs energy through their own hands, working entirely in the energy field without actually touching the physical body, to increase or decrease energy to bring it into balance.

Healing Touch and Reiki. Healing Touch, developed by Janet Mentgen, RN, is similar to Therapeutic Touch, also using hand-scanning to feel the energies, but it involves actually placing the hands on the chakras. Reiki, developed by Dr. Usui in Japan, involves placing the hands directly on the chakras and other parts of the body.

Combined Methods

Vibrational Healing. The Vibrational Healer balances the body's electromagnetic energy using vibratory tools such as color, light, sound (toning), gemstones, and aromatic oils.

Vibrational Alignment™. In this form of Vibrational Healing which I have developed, the practitioner uses their hand or a long clear quartz crystal to feel the spin of subtle energies at each of the chakras to determine: where the client is holding unfinished business (first and second chakras); issues of self-worth and fear of power (third chakra); unresolved traumas from the past (fourth chakra); and sources of mental and spiritual confusion (higher chakras). Once the reason for the illness is understood, the practitioner uses the vibratory tools to help the body find its own healthy harmonic resonance.

BOOKS BY THE CROSSING PRESS

BOOKS BY THE CROSSING PRESS

Pocket Guide to Numerology
By Alan Oken
ISBN 0-89594-826-5

Pocket Guide to Self Hypnosis
By Adam Burke, Ph. D.
ISBN 0-89594-824-9

Pocket Guide to Shamanism
By Tom Cowan
ISBN 0-89594-845-1

Pocket Guide to the 12-Steps
By Kathleen S.
ISBN 0-89594-864-8

Pocket Guide to The Tarot
By Alan Oken
ISBN 0-89594-822-2

Pocket Guide to Visualization
By Helen Graham
ISBN 0-89594-885-0

Pocket Guide to Wicca
By Paul Tuitean & Estelle
Daniels
ISBN 0-89594-904-0

Pocket Herbal Reference Guide
By Debra St. Claire
ISBN 0-89594-568-1

To receive a current catalog from The Crossing Press
please call toll-free, 800-777-1048.
Visit our Web site on the Internet: www. crossingpress.com